Prayer

Dynamics

From Inspiration to

Transformation

A 31 Day Devotional Journey

Marsha Headley

Prayer Dynamics: From Inspiration to Transformation, A 31 Day Devotional Journey

© Copyright 2016 by Marsha Headley

Published by Marsha Headley

2nd Printing

White House, TN

ISBN: **978-0-578-18489-0**

Contact Author at: mheadleymail@yahoo.com

Cover design by:

Jonathan Isaac May

Printed in the United States of America

Acknowledgements

No story is complete without a journey. No writer ever publishes without much support and help. This book certainly gives evidence of those truths. There are innumerable people who have influenced and inspired me along the way. It is with a grateful heart that I share my sincere appreciation and thanks to so many that have impacted this writing:

To my precious parents, Ruth and Paul Radke, now in Heaven, who not only prayed for me but also modeled prayer before me. Dad, thank you for the words you spoke to me. God has brought them to fulfillment.

To my family and friends, many who read my manuscript in its infancy and urged me on to completion. You have been a tremendous encouragement through your prayers, your pertinent suggestions, and your loving support: Bethany Metzger, Bobby Radke, Robert Storey, Mark Oberbeck, Paul Radke, Joy and Gregg Headley, Wade Jones, Mindy Brose, Pattie Manz, Linda McCreight, Marie Segura, Tammy Cascio, Anne Bosman, Margaret Beyer, Susan Bailey, Anabelle Treuil, Martha Posey, Natomi Hoots, Sierra Snapp, Stephanie Jackson, Dana Manuel, Jeannie Snell, Barb Rich, and Rhonda Johnson.

To friends and family who gave hours of editing assistance: Irmi Mace, Sheila Harper, Brenda Walden, Kitty Foth-Regnar, Dr. Chere Blair, Carlene Withers, Fannie Mae Hall, Nancy Vyvyan, Bobbie Spitz, Dr. Connie Lawrence-Hurst, and Shirley Speer. You have all contributed to this writing and to me as a writer. I am sincerely grateful!

To the friends, too many to mention, who have prayed for me and for the completion of this book. May God bless your lives immensely!

To my family for their input, love, and prayer support. Thank you for allowing me to be part of your lives and for giving me the privilege to share your stories. You are an invaluable part of me and I love you dearly! My daughter Bethany and son-in-law, Matt Metzger, My granddaughter Tuesday, and grandson, Miles, our newest arrival. My son Stephen and daughter-in-law, Julie. My siblings: Ruth Radke-Smith, Paula Oberbeck, Kathy Storey, and Chip Radke. My in-law parents, Jimmie Ruth and Lamar Headley

To my wonderful and amazing husband, Bruce. You have encouraged me when I felt incompetent and spurred me on when I wanted to quit. You have lifted my load so I to could follow my gifts and callings. I thank God for the precious gift you are to my life.

Thank you so much to my precious Lord and Savior, Jesus, to whom all praise and glory are due. You have been so faithful to encourage, to guide, to help, and to speak to me on this journey of life. Words could never express my love and gratitude for all you have done for me!

To Bruce,
You are a God-given completion of my life.
Your model of great faith has always been an inspiration and at times a challenge
to catch up.
I love you. I always will.

Table of Contents

Preface

The Most Important Prayer

When we pray, God never says, "Who are you and what do you want?!!" The Bible says God is always listening to our calls for help and our cries to Him. Amazingly, He knows every detail about us even before we are born. He knows our words before we say them. He knows our thoughts before we think them (Psalm 139). Jesus said our Heavenly Father even counts the numbers of the hairs on our heads. God, however, has more than an immense interest or liking for us, His creation.

Scripture reveals that God actually desires to have a personal friendship with each of us every day. He wants this relationship, not just for a lifetime, but for eternity, ensuring a place in Heaven for us. It is for this reason, He sent Jesus to Earth. God wanted you and me to understand He loves us very much—so much, in fact, that He allowed His only Son to die on a cross to pay the price for our sins.

If we want to be effective in our prayers, we must know our Heavenly Father and experience this new encounter with Him. This relationship is not born out of church membership, though it is important to gather with other people who believe the Bible and are committed to following Christ. It is only through Jesus, however, not through a church that we are saved.

If you want to experience God in this way and be assured of your eternity in Heaven, pray this most important prayer. It is based in Scripture, it is life transforming, and it will open the door to a new relationship with your Heavenly Father:

> **"Dear Father God,**
> **Thank you for your Son, Jesus, who died for my sins and rose**
> **from the dead. I repent of my past, and I ask for your help to**

forsake my sin. I receive Jesus as my Lord and Savior. I choose to follow your Word and your plan for my life. Guide me, and help me to do your will. In Jesus Name. Amen."

- *John 3:16 For God so loved the world, that he gave his only Son, that whoever believes in him should not perish but have eternal life.*
- *I John 1:9 If we confess our sins, he is faithful and just to forgive us our sins and to cleanse us from all unrighteousness.*
- *Romans 10:9 If you confess with your mouth that Jesus is Lord and believe in your heart that God raised him from the dead, you will be saved. For with the heart one believes and is justified, and with the mouth one confesses and is saved.*
- *John 1:12 But to all who did receive him, who believed in his name, he gave the right to become children of God.*
- *I John 5:11-13 And this is the testimony that God gave us eternal life, and this life is in his Son. Whoever has the Son has life, whoever does not have the Son of God does not have life. I write these things to you who believe in the name of the Son of God that you may know that you have eternal life.*

Introduction

I can identify with Abraham's wife, Sarah. I laughed, too—no, not about having a baby—but about words that seemed outrageous to me. They were from my dad. He looked at me as if he himself was surprised at the revelation he had just received: "Marsha," he announced, "you are supposed to write a book! Not just one book but, I believe, several." I chuckled respectfully and said, "Dad, you have never even read anything I have written." My words did not dissuade him, though. He reaffirmed that he sincerely believed it was God's plan for me. The truth was, I didn't like to write. But I did not forget his words. Though I protested, his declaration resounded deep inside of me as God's truth.

Like Sarah, I received a second God-given insight about this "baby" you hold in your hand. It came from my friend and mentor, Anne Bosman. "Marsha, God is raising up a prayer ministry through you," she announced in her South African accent as I sat wearily at the piano at the end of a church service. Dumbfounded, this time, I didn't laugh. I just inwardly groaned (not the spiritual kind). I could not imagine directing one more thing. I was already overloaded and overwhelmed from my church duties and speaking opportunities. Anne's words seemed incredulous to me since I felt like the most unlikely candidate. My own life felt very prayer challenged. However, she, too, had that surprised look of revelation. Like Jesus' mother, Mary, I pondered those things in my heart.

In time, those prophetic seeds began to germinate within me and here you sit with this book in your hand. Truly a miracle!

Speaking of miracles...

The Bible is full of them. The truths of the Scripture are underscored and brought to life by those miracles. What about miracles today? Did God change? Did Jesus leave us with just a dried up riverbed of rhetoric? What about the power of the Holy

Spirit demonstrated by the early church? Are miracles still possible, or are they just for generations of the past?

My life has been inspired and transformed by miracles...miracles in my family, miracles in our lives, miracles in our ministry. Does it mean I have not had—and still have—questions when things don't turn out as I had prayed, hoped, and expected? Yes, just like you, there are things I do not understand; I, too, have faced disillusionment. However, those issues will not stop me from believing for more miracles.

Here is where prayer comes in. If we are going to see miracles, we must continually seek God for His intervention in our everyday lives. We must not be afraid to have faith. We must take God at His Word and hold His promises before Him. His Word stands true through the ages.

Though times have changed, culture has changed—even we have changed—but Jesus has not and will never change! This book is intended to inspire you to get back to what God has called you to—prayer. Then He can get back to what He has promised to do—miracles.

- *Hebrews 13:8 Jesus Christ is the same yesterday, today, and forever.*
- *Jeremiah 33:3 Call to me, and I will answer you, and show you great and mighty things, which you do not know.*
- *John 14:12 Truly, truly, I say to you, whoever believes in me will also do the works that I do; and greater works than these will he do, because I am going to the Father.*
- *Ephesians 3:20-21 Now to Him who is able to do exceedingly abundantly above all that we ask or think, according to the power that works in us, to Him be glory in the church by Christ Jesus to all generations, forever and ever. Amen.*

SECTION 1

WHY SHOULD I PRAY?

We All Need Prayer

Psalm 145:18,19 The Lord is near to all who call on him, to all who call on him in truth. He fulfills the desire of those who fear him; He also hears their cry and saves them.

"The greatest thing anyone can do for God and man is pray. The great people of the earth today are the people who pray. I do not mean those who talk about prayer; nor those who say they believe in prayer; nor yet those who can explain about prayer; but I mean these people who take time to pray."

–S.D. Gordon

In the history of humankind, no one had broken the 4-minute mile, that is, until Roger Bannister. Physicians said the human heart couldn't stand it. They said it would explode. But on May 6, 1954, Roger Bannister broke through. Since his victory, others have excelled past him, making the record 3 minutes, 43 seconds at the time of this writing.

Another challenge stands ready to be broken. Studies on prayer give evidence the average Christian prays 5 minutes—that's 5 minutes a week, not 5 minutes a day—hardly enough time to pray a blessing over the food and say, "Now I lay me down to sleep...," when our head hits the pillow at night. Our lives are very busy, and it is reflected in our lack of prayer.

"When you pray..." Matthew 6:5 begins, affirming Jesus expected us to pray. Why, then, is prayer one of the most difficult challenges of the Christian life? Perhaps it is because prayer requires our time and commitment. It requires putting aside our agenda for God's agenda.

Prayer, like the discipline of eating a healthy diet, needs lifelong attention to be maintained but pays off in the long run. If we are faithful to pray, the dividends multiply exponentially for our loved ones, our world, and ourselves as we move toward eternity.

Some people say prayer doesn't work; miracles don't exist. But the truth is, *none of us would exist without miracles and none of us would have any miracles without prayer!* God is a supernatural God and He proves it time after time through His divine intervention in our lives. Through prayer, He enables us to be His partners in miracles. We all need prayer, and I am living proof that prayer works. Let me give you an example of what I mean:

We were pastoring in Birmingham, Alabama. One Sunday night after church, we went to have supper with our evangelist, Frank Matthews, at a local restaurant. Frank, who was then working among the gangs in the inner city of Birmingham, had been miraculously saved and mercifully delivered out of generations of the Black Mafia. His transformation was so dramatic that he was ultimately released from a long and deserved prison sentence.

From the moment Frank walked into the restaurant that night, he was troubled that there was a suspicious-looking man dressed in a trench coat talking on the phone. Frank suspected he was not really on the phone at all but was, in Frank's words, "up to no good."

We were seated near the back of the sparsely populated restaurant when Frank began sharing, "If the suburban church does not reach out to the inner city, the violence of the inner city will be on the doorsteps of the suburban church."

Minutes later, five masked gunmen entered the front doors. Immediately, each one targeted a different place in the restaurant. It happened so fast; we all sat in stunned silence. "Give me your money!" the gunman at our table demanded. My husband, Bruce, cooperated as best he could with the three dollars in his pocket. His coat was in the booth not far away but the gunman wouldn't let him get up. Frank was not so amenable. "I'm not giving you anything! Everything I have belongs to Jesus!" he retorted. I held my breath. The gunman must have had a praying mother or grandmother because he responded, "Ok, man, I'm goin' to cut you some slack."

After holding up all the customers and workers in the restaurant, the men forced us at gunpoint—fifteen adults and our two small children, Bethany, 6, and Stephen, 4, into the restaurant's walk-in freezer. We all remained huddled in the freezer for about ten minutes in obedience to the last instructions of the gang leader. Frank, however, climbed over all of us to get out so he could get a good look at the getaway vehicle.

"Frightened" doesn't even come close to describing my feelings in those moments of waiting. Though I had memorized many scriptures, even a number of Bible chapters, not one would come to mind because of the intense panic I felt. All I could say was "angels, angels" under my breath.

With tremendous trepidation, we finally walked out of the freezer. We prayed with those who had been accosted in the restaurant with us, while waiting for the police to arrive. As Bruce led in prayer, I couldn't help but wonder, "Lord, who was praying for us?"

After the police reports were done, we called our families to share our scary saga. No one said anything about a burden of prayer that night, though our parents and families are people of prayer and have been prompted of the Lord to pray for us at many critical times.

It was not until a few days later, our next door neighbor and church member, Martha Posey, resolved the mystery. She shared with us how she had felt very impressed of the Lord that weekend to pray for our safety. She kept telling the Lord we were pastors and had plenty of people praying for us. Unable to move past the prevailing impression, she interceded for us. God heard Martha's prayers that Sunday night and rescued our family.

We stand connected

Our lives are supernaturally intertwined. The Apostle Paul said we are "members one of another." Our prayers matter more than we realize for our families, our neighbors, our churches, our nation, and our world. God wants to intervene in your life and mine, even in the life of humankind on this earth. Most often, He does it through prayer.

True Story: Our good friend Norm Correll and his family were missionaries to East Africa. Returning from a ministry endeavor by boat, Norm and his family, along with another missionary, Del Kingsriter and his family, were all attacked by killer bees. They were each stung hundreds of times. Del had the presence of mind to pull the boat up to a nearby village where the people rallied to help by building a big fire to deter the bees. Norm's wife, Norma, who was allergic to bee stings, suffered the worst. She lay at the point of death, not breathing, her skin already blue.

On the other side of the world in Iowa, a young 9-year-old boy tried several times to get his dad's attention during their evening family prayer and devotions. Finally, the child blurted out, "Dad, if we don't pray now, that missionary family whose pictures are on our refrigerator are going to die!" They stopped and fervently prayed for Norm and his family.

The story of the family's intercession remained unknown until a couple of years later when Norm was on furlough speaking at a family camp in his home state, Nebraska. That night he shared the story of the killer bee attack. He testified of God's supernatural intervention and healing miracle for Norma, their family, and the other missionaries with them, ultimately impacting the African village for God.

At the end of the service, the grandmother of the 9-year-old boy came up to Norm. She recounted her experience of spending Christmas with her son's family in Iowa two years earlier. She gave details of their evening devotions and her grandson's unusual plea to pray for missionaries in a life and death situation. After comparing the date and time in this grandmother's diary, they realized the family's prayers in Iowa occurred at the exact time of the killer bee attack on the other side of the world.

SOMETHING TO THINK ABOUT: Consider the effect of the prayers of those at the home of Mary, John Mark's mother, in Acts, chapter 12. As they cried out to the Lord to save Peter—chained and sitting on death row in a dank prison cell—God answered and sent an angel to release him. How can your prayers make a difference in others' lives? Be sensitive to listen and obey the voice of the Spirit of God. Our prayers are sometimes the difference between life and death.

PRAYER EXERCISE: Make a decision today to break the 5-minute prayer mile marker by praying every day. Start this day by thanking God for the different ways that prayer, whether your own or someone else's, has benefited your life. Start a list of people who need your prayers and call their names and needs out to God. Keep the list in your prayer journal (or your smart phone notes) to pray over daily.

Psalm 55:16-17 But I call on God, and the Lord will rescue me. Morning, noon, and night I cry out in my distress, and the Lord hears my voice.

The Benefits of Prayer

James 5:16 (NLT) The earnest prayer of a righteous person has great power and produces wonderful results.

Psalm 32:6 Therefore, let everyone who is godly offer prayer to you at a time when you may be found; surely in the rush of great waters, they shall not reach him.

"We get distracted from God and irritable with Him while He continues to say to us, "Look to Me, and be saved" Our difficulties, our trials, and our worries about tomorrow all vanish when we look to God."

-Oswald Chambers

If prayer is so important, then why don't we pray? My life has been spared countless times through prayer. So why, then, was prayer my greatest challenge? How could that be? I was a pastor's wife. I was raised in a pastor's home.

One day, as I was pondering my prayer-challenged schedule, the Lord said to me, "There are two major reasons you don't pray." That got my attention so I listened. "The first reason is you don't think prayer makes a difference." Of course I protested, but the Lord clearly spoke and said, "No! If you really believed it made a difference, then you would pray more." Ouch! The truth hurt! James 5:16 rang clearly in my thoughts: *"The effectual fervent prayer of a righteous man (or woman) avails much."*

Further, the Lord spoke, "The other reason you don't pray more is you think you can do it without Me." In my mind, I saw myself going from daylight to dark doing all kinds of good works for the church and for the Kingdom without sufficient prayer. I realized to God it was like saying, "I got this!" Jesus clearly said in John 15:5b, *"For apart from me, you can do nothing."* That means zero.

Zilch.

The Father reminded me of the many times Jesus separated Himself for prayer. Amazingly, three times in the book of John, Jesus explained He could do nothing of Himself but only that which He heard from His Father. If Jesus, the Son of God, could not operate autonomously, how could I ever accomplish anything without the help of the Father?

Prayerlessness is a form of self-pride

The root of prayerlessness is pride because it indicates we feel we are sufficient without God's help, capable of doing things on our own. The Bible says, "Humble yourself under the mighty hand of God..." (1Peter 5:6). Prayer is one of the most important ways we can humble ourselves before God.

Prayer provides communication and direction

Prayer is the primary way we communicate and learn to hear our Father's heart. Prayer helps to bring us into alignment with our Father's will. It is often in times of prayer that God discloses His plan and purpose for our lives.

Many times we have pieces of our lives that don't make sense. Like a giant unassembled puzzle, our lives seem random and out of order; the pieces lie askew on the table before us, and we struggle even to find the starting piece. God, however, knows what the final product is supposed to look like. He has seen the picture on the box, so to speak, because He made the puzzle. It is only through time spent with Him that we find out how our picture, one piece at a time, fits into place for the fulfillment of our destiny and God's bigger picture at large.

Prayer is a lifeline

God is our source of life. Like a spiritual umbilical cord, prayer keeps our hearts and thoughts connected to God. It is only *"In Him we live and move and have our being"* (Acts 17:28a).

The world provides a constant disconnect in terms of our spiritual wellbeing. Media, daily tasks, problems, and relationships bombard us. Prayer helps us to find a place of constancy in God, through Christ, who brings wholeness and focus for our lives.

True Story: During our first pastorate in Dothan, Alabama, Bruce developed a severe headache that would not go away. He began to have other symptoms indicating his need for medical attention. We took him to the emergency room, and he was admitted to the hospital. Tests revealed he had viral meningitis.

Bruce continued with such a severe headache that when the doctor did a spinal tap, normally a very painful procedure, Bruce never felt it. His sugar level spiked to 300 while his blood pressure plummeted. Our families, our friends, and our church were praying for him. In the middle of the night, desperate for relief, Bruce pleaded with the Lord to give him 5 minutes of sleep without pain. God answered his prayer in that miraculous moment and completely healed him. Bruce went right to sleep and awakened totally well the next morning with all of his vital signs returned to normal. He was released from the hospital on Friday and preached in our church on Sunday.

SOMETHING TO THINK ABOUT: Much scientific study has been done on prayer in the last 10 years. Scientist and researcher Andrew Newburg found there was an actual beneficial change in brain scans when subjects in his study began praying. Instead of the brain's frontal lobes increasing in blood flow, the blood flow actually decreased to a more restful state when his subjects prayed.

> "For them it's the spirit of God which is moving through them. I can't prove that or disprove that on the basis of a brain scan, but I can see the changes that are going on in the brain while they're engaged in this very, very powerful and very deep spiritual practice... It certainly looks like the way the brain is put together makes it very easy for human beings to have religious and spiritual experiences."[1]

God created us with a divine capacity to interact and communicate with Him. While secular scientists and humanists draw their own conclusions, a great wealth of research shows prayer is beneficial to our bodies, our minds, and our emotions.

However, there is something significant this research does not show, and that is how prayer also brings results as God responds in answer to our requests.

PRAYER EXERCISE: Pray for God to reveal the root of your own prayerlessness. Repent to God for your neglect, and request His help for the development of a meaningful and effective prayer life. In your prayer journal, make a list of mindsets and obstacles, which have previously prevented you so you will not fall prey to them. Ask God to give you strategies to overcome them.

Psalm 25:9 He leads the humble in what is right, and teaches the humble his way.

Psalm 17:6 (NLT) I am praying to you because I know you will answer, O God. Bend down and listen as I pray.

The Most Important Reason to Pray

Isaiah 55:6 Seek the Lord while he may be found; call upon him while he is near.

James 4:8a Draw near to God and He will draw near to you.

"If there were no devil there would be no difficulty in prayer. It is the evil one's chief aim to make prayer impossible."

-unknown (Dick Eastman, No Easy Road)

"It seems that before the Lord can do anything in the earth, a man must ask him."

John Wesley

There are times in the life of every parent that we have to use our last resort, our God-given executive power—"Because I said so!" This proclamation has usually come after lengthy explanations of our wisdom and reasoning to the incessant "why" of our 2-year-old or our insistent teen. This same frustration is perhaps what our Heavenly Father feels with us when it comes to our own, "Why do I have to pray?" The most important reason? Because He said so.

I used to wonder, "If God, who is omniscient, knows our needs even before we ask, what's the big deal about prayer?" Then God began to show me why prayer on our part is a necessity. Let's start at the beginning when Adam and Eve "voted" God out of the garden:

God had everything beautifully arranged for our initial ancestors to live in paradise forever. But they said, "No, thank you. We would rather do it our way." Likewise, we have individually and corporately continued their pattern by eradicating God from our lives. Consider the resounding echo of defiance against Heaven's authority in the ruling of *Roe vs. Wade*, prayer removed from our schools, the Ten

Commandments eliminated from public buildings, and the Supreme Court decisions which defy biblical morality.

The problem of evil

As a result of our decisions and their consequences, people get disillusioned with God. They lose their faith because they have no explanation for all of the injustice, evil, and chaos in our world. Recently, I read a magazine that said more college students walk away from their faith because of "the problem of evil," than for any other reason.

What most people don't realize is that when Adam and Eve chose their plan over God's design, they opened the door to evil by sanctioning a rogue ruler. Satan is a thief whose order of the day is to steal, kill, and destroy. He wreaks havoc in relationships, destroys marriages and families, and abuses innocent children. He personally instituted famine, disaster, sickness, and disease. Worse yet, Satan daily frames God and whispers, "He did it," into the hearts of the unsuspecting.

Jesus' response in the third test of the Temptation gave evidence of this fact of Satan's rulership on this earth. There on the mountaintop, Satan offered Jesus the kingdoms of this world if only our Lord would bow down and worship him. Jesus responded to the Tempter by saying, "It is written." But did He counter Satan's claim to this world by saying, *"The earth is the Lord's, and the fullness thereof, the world and those who dwell therein"* (Psalm 24:1)? No, He did not. Jesus only declared, *"You shall worship the Lord your God, and Him only shall you serve"* (Matthew 4:10b). Why did our Lord not contest the Enemy's bold assertion of ownership? Here's why: Satan could offer up the kingdoms of this world on a tempting platter to Jesus because it was his to give...but only for a time.

> "God ultimately reigns over the entire universe. But for the moment there appears to be one piece of turf in the cosmos that is not operating under His reign. ...the dominion over this piece of real estate was forfeited to a character who himself had rejected the reign of God somewhere before the realm of time as we know it."[2]

24

The invitation

IT IS FOR THIS REASON THAT PRAYER IS SO IMPORTANT. Prayer invites God back into our world, back into our nation, back into our schools, back into our homes, and back into our lives. Prayer is our way of welcoming God back into the world He created but which rejected Him.

Prayer is our way of reestablishing His authorship and rulership in our lives. It is how we accomplish seeing His will done on this Earth as it is in Heaven. No chanting, no rituals, no sacrifice. Just prayer. Prayer is the only invitation God will accept.

> *Psalm 27:7,8 (NLT) Hear me as I pray, O Lord. Be merciful and answer me! My heart has heard you say, "Come and talk with me." And my heart responds, "Lord I am coming."*

True Stories: Our lives have been affected generationally through prayer. My maternal grandmother was healed of tuberculosis as her family gathered around her in prayer just prior to being admitted to a sanitarium. Bruce's grandmother was healed of life-threatening injuries from a car accident. My mother was healed of cervical cancer and breast cancer. My father was healed of pneumonia of such severity that his doctor did not believe he would live through the night. Bruce's mother was healed of polio and though the doctor said she would never walk without evidence of it, she walks perfectly. These stories are true and reflect the impact of prayer to our God who hears and answers.

SOMETHING TO THINK ABOUT: The Apostle Paul said, *"Satan, who is the god of this world has blinded the eyes of those who don't believe"* (2 Corinthians 4:4, NLT). Consider also that even the natural realm has been affected and continues to suffer under the curse (Romans 8:20-22). These things happened as a result of human choices.

When Jesus came, He did more than even the score. Jesus exposed Satan's assignment against us to steal, kill, and destroy. He came so we could have abundant life. Jesus revealed in the flesh the very names and nature of God:

- I am the Lord your Savior (Isaiah 43:11; 2 Timothy 1:10).

- I am the Lord your healer (Exodus 15:26; 1 Peter 2:24).

- I am the Lord your provider (Genesis 22:14; John 6:35).

- I am the Lord your peace (Judges 6:24; John 14:27).

- I am the Lord your defender (Psalm 18:1,2; 1 John 2:1).

- I am the Lord your righteousness (Jeremiah 33:16; 2 Corinthians 5:21).

- I am the Lord your constant companion (Deuteronomy 31:6; Hebrews 13:5).

As we pray, we are appropriating God's provision for us through Christ. We are also, by our choice to pray, countering Satan's takeover in the lives of our families and even in the lives of people we may never meet. Be encouraged. Scripture shows we win!

PRAYER EXERCISE: Identify ways the Enemy is using his schemes against your loved ones. As you pray, ask God to expose the lies of Satan, and reveal the truth of God to them. Pray that God will break the assignment of the Enemy. Proclaim the name of God that fits the need of your loved one, as in Lord you said, "I am the Lord, _____'s Healer".

> *1 John 4:4 Little children, you are from God and have overcome them, for he who is in you is greater than he who is in the world.*
>
> *Matthew 6:10 Your kingdom come, your will be done, on earth as it is in heaven.*

Anyone Can Pray

Psalm 18:6 In my distress I called upon the Lord; to my God I cried for help. From his temple he heard my voice, and my cry to him reached his ears.

Psalm 34:17 When the righteous cry for help, the Lord hears and delivers them out of all their troubles.

"A child exhibits a magnificent boldness to ask! Our Lord said, '…unless you…become as little children…' Ask and God will do."

- Oswald Chambers, My Utmost for His Highest

"Gary was the bestest caterpillar I never known!" cried Tuesday, my 3-year-old granddaughter. She was mourning the death of her friend, a cabbage looper that we had discovered on the collard greens in my garden. Despite my warning, Tuesday had made the tragic decision to give Gary a bath. Though I was glad to be rid of the destructive little creature, he had become a faithful friend of a few hours for Tuesday.

After her sorrowful outburst she disappeared into the other room, I thought, to go play. My daughter, Bethany, came to me moments later saying, "Mom, you have got to come see Tuesday!" We quickly scurried through the house and found Tuesday in her little play tent crying out to God with a loud tearful voice, "Oh Lord, pleeease touch Gary! Please, please, pleeease touch Gary!!! He was a good caterpillar, Lord," she continued. "He was the bestest caterpillar there ever was! Please, please, touch Gary!!! In your name, it's done." She continued her loud pleading until she heard our hushed efforts to find the video camera, at which point she came out a little embarrassed, wiping tears from her eyes.

Tuesday's intercession surprised both her mother and me. Was this the same little 3-year-old we regularly had to coax to pray, whether at bedtime, mealtime, or morning prayers? Was this the same little girl who prayed using her whiniest, most resistant voice unless instructed to do otherwise? Who taught her that prayer could make a difference? How did she know how to intercede so intensely?

Prayer principles

Amazingly, Tuesday enacted two important principles of prayer. Consider using them in your prayer time:

1. Pour out your heart to God. *"O my people, trust in him at all times. Pour out your heart to him, for God is our refuge"* (Psalm 62:8, NLT).
2. Tell your needs to God. *"Don't worry about anything, instead, pray about everything. Tell God what you need, and thank him for all he has done"* (Philippians 4:6, NLT).

We didn't realize the depth of Tuesday's understanding about prayer and intercession until that moment. It was evident the problem was not in the "know how" but the "want to." She had known how to pray but just didn't choose to do so until the situation seemed to necessitate it.

It is true we all feel incompetent to pray at times. Though there are ways we can learn to pray better, the truth is a certain amount of "know how" is in all of us. Why does it take facing a difficult situation for most of us to turn to God for help? Is it any wonder God allows you and me to go through challenging times? Often, it is the only way He can turn us toward Himself in order to reach our hearts.

Our prayers have purpose

Prayer is not a meaningless exercise in futility. God tells us to cry out to Him because He will listen and answer. Our prayers do make a difference to God for the situations about which we are praying.

When we look around and see the times we live in, the hurting people all around us, the state of our broken world, our hearts must respond. Like Tuesday, desperate times call for desperate measures. It's time to pray! In the midst of life's chaos, prayer is the only solution.

1 Peter 4:7(NLT) The end of the world is coming soon. Therefore, be earnest and disciplined in your prayers.

True Story: Our friends are missionaries in a "sensitive" nation. During the wife's pregnancy, the Lord had provided excellent prenatal care through a missionary doctor in country. Since there was a very high mortality rate of both mothers and infants in the local hospitals due to terrible hygiene and improper medical practices, they, with the encouragement of the missionary doctor, made the decision to go to Istanbul, Turkey, to have their baby delivered.

As the missionaries were making efforts to get everything in place, they could feel the governmental resistance at every turn. When the day came for them to fly to Istanbul, they had their tickets and paperwork in order and in hand. However, as they went through the first checkpoint, it appeared the agent was not going to let them board the plane to leave. After a few heart-pounding moments, the agent deferred to the person with greater authority who was at the next checkpoint. Our missionary friend shared with me that in that instant, he felt God tell him to pray for his wife and child to be invisible to the person at the next gate. On the other side of the world, his aunt, though unaware of their critical situation, also felt led by God to pray the same prayer—specifically, that they would become invisible. Later, during the Wednesday night church service where the aunt was in attendance, the pastor had the congregation join together in prayer for her missionary nephew and his family.

Back at the airport, the tension mounted as the missionaries arrived at the final checkpoint. The person at the gate meticulously greeted every man, woman, child, and even babies who were boarding the plane, a customary procedure there. Miraculously, when the missionaries walked up, this woman spoke only to the husband. She seemed totally unaware of his very pregnant wife and young child. In fact, this gate agent looked right past them as if she did not even see them. This missionary family boarded the plane with praises to God in their hearts and quietly on their lips. Their prayers, and the prayers of a church on the other side of the world had been answered. Our missionary friends flew on to Istanbul where their baby was born healthy and without endangerment.

SOMETHING TO THINK ABOUT: Prayer has no time, place, or space boundaries. We can cry out to God at any time, in any place. God is able to move on behalf of the person next to us or to intervene in a crisis in the most obscure corner of the earth. Prayer requires no formal education, no extra finances, no special connections, or political influence. The ground is level at the cross and in the prayer closet.

PRAYER EXERCISE: Pour out your heart to God and tell Him your needs. As you release those things into His loving hands, trust Him to begin the work that is needed. Then pray that God will begin to open your eyes of compassion to the needs around you. Ask the Lord to show you what you can do to make a difference in your neighborhood, your church, and your community. Make a list in your prayer journal of needs that you see, and ask God to show you what you can do to be His hands extended.

> *Matthew 9:36-38 When he saw the crowds, he had compassion on them, because they were harassed and helpless, like sheep without a shepherd. Then he said to his disciples, "The harvest is plentiful, but the laborers are few; therefore pray earnestly to the Lord of the harvest to send out laborers into his harvest."*

Cultivating a Desire for Prayer

Psalm 42:1,2 As a deer pants for flowing streams, so pants my soul for you, O God. My soul thirsts for God, for the living God. When shall I come and appear before God?

Psalm 130:6 My soul waits for the Lord more than watchmen for the morning, more than watchmen for the morning.

"We look upon prayer simply as a means of getting things for ourselves, but the biblical purpose of prayer is that we may get to know God Himself."

-Oswald Chambers, My Utmost for His Highest

Is it possible to come to the place where we want to pray? Certain people in my life have made me "thirsty" for God as I sensed the close communication they had with Him and yearned for that close relationship in my own life. The memory of my mom and dad who prayed faithfully for us, their five children, has inspired and compelled me to pray. But none is more attractive to me than our Lord Himself.

Jesus set an example for us of prayer. Prayer was a way of life for Him. In fact, the Bible says Jesus actually *sought* lonely places to pray (Luke 5:16). That is hard to for me to understand since lonely places have never been my favorites.

I do have some questions:

1. Did Jesus want to pray because He was weary of the crowds of people, or needed a break from His petty, imperfect disciples?

2. Did He even need to pray? Most of us pray for answers. He already knew the answers *before* the questions. Jesus was God in the flesh. He had a direct line to God already, didn't He? As to needing help, He had "All power in Heaven and on

31

Earth" that had been given to Him. More than twelve legions of angels were poised and ready for His command.

3. Was Jesus homesick? I once met a nurse who died and went to Heaven for just a minute or two. She missed Heaven so much that when she returned to her earthly body, she was depressed for 6 months.

Jesus must have missed Heaven, also. The beauty of perfection, the sounds of constant praise, the rapturous music—even more, though, I believe He must have missed the intimate fellowship He enjoyed with His Father.

Fellowship is a reason for prayer

Prayer, for most of us, is an endeavor by which we seek God's hand to move in our situation. But fellowship is an endeavor by which we seek God's heart, like a special meeting with a dear friend or loved one. It is a time when we not only speak *to Him*, but we give our Lord the freedom to speak *to us*. Initially, this may seem awkward since you are learning a new way to experience God. The Lord speaks to each of us uniquely, so it is a journey that will take your time and His direction.

Consider the benefits of fellowship with God:

- Fellowship with God makes prayer a celebration rather than a requirement.
- Fellowship with God creates intimacy, connecting our hearts to Him.
- Fellowship with God enlightens our minds to His will and plan for us.
- Fellowship with God provides a place of partnership rather than just a platform for petition.

The void

We get busy with our lives, our families, our jobs—even our church activities—and it becomes easy to overlook or even withdraw from our times of fellowship with our Father. However, there is a vacuum when we don't take time to be alone with God. After all, we were created to have fellowship with Him.

Each of us has an inner sanctuary where the Savior wants not only to dwell but also to fellowship. Jesus spoke of this in *Revelation 3:20: "Behold I stand at the door and knock. If anyone hears my voice and opens the door, I will come in to him and eat with him and he with me."* It is an invitation that has your name on it.

> "Let us occupy ourselves, entirely in knowing God. The more we know Him, the more we will desire to know Him. As love increases with knowledge, the more we know God, the more we will truly love Him. We will learn to love Him equally in times of distress or in times of great joy."[3]

True Story: Shortly after the iron curtain fell, Bruce took a team of more than twenty people on a trip to do evangelism in Russia. Though they had obtained all of the government paperwork necessary for their evangelism crusades, they were commanded to stop and were placed under house arrest.

It was during this rather tense downtime that Bruce gave his team a prayer assignment. He asked that they remain in the meeting room for an hour but requested they speak to no one except God. Each person was allowed only a notebook, a pen, and their Bible.

When the team meeting reconvened an hour later, they were all amazed at how God had spoken to each one of their hearts. The Lord had given one individual a song, another a poem, and others received revelations from the Scriptures. All had a story and an encounter with God to share.

SOMETHING TO THINK ABOUT: According to Scripture, Jesus holds many keys—the keys to the Kingdom, the key of the house of David, the keys of hell and death—but only we have the key to open the door of our hearts. The doorknob is on our side. When we open that door by receiving Him, Jesus comes in to fellowship with us.

One of the ways we cultivate fellowship with God is the same way we cultivate fellowship with our spouse, our children, or our friend—by setting aside blocks of time to meet together.

Another way we nurture fellowship is by going to special places where we have chosen to connect, celebrate, or vacation. These concepts of special time and special place can be used to develop our fellowship time with God. He is just waiting for us to carve out a place for Him in our schedules.

Consider the words of the beautiful hymn, *In the Garden*. They perfectly demonstrate the fellowship our Lord desires to have with each of us.

> "I come to the garden alone, while the dew is still on the roses. And the voice I hear falling on my ear, the Son of God discloses. And He walks with me and He talks with me, and He tells me I am His own. And the joy we share as we tarry there, none other has ever known."[4]   *-by C. Austin Miles*

PRAYER EXERCISE: Choose a special time and place where you meet with Jesus just for fellowship today or another time this week. Bring your Bible, and ask Him to speak to you as you read and pray. Take along a notebook to write the things you hear or feel an impression about. Consider doing this on a daily or a weekly basis. Make a "date" with the Lord part of your regular prayer routine.

> *Psalm 25:14 The friendship of the Lord is for those who fear him, and he makes known to them his covenant.*

> *James 2:23 And the Scripture was fulfilled that says, "Abraham believed God, and it was counted to him as righteousness"—and he was called a friend of God.*

SECTION 2

HOW CAN I GET GOD TO NOTICE?

Faithfulness Matters to God

Acts 10:4 (NKJV) ...your prayers and alms have come up for a memorial before God.

Romans 12:12 (NIV) Be joyful in hope, patient in affliction, faithful in prayer.

"Don't pray when you feel like it. Have an appointment with the Lord and keep it. A man is powerful on his knees."

-Corrie ten Boom

A friend of mine had a dream that he was sitting above the Earth, accompanied by an angel. It was a nighttime neighborhood scene. All throughout the city in different places were beams of light that went up to the heavens. My friend asked the angel the significance of the beams and why they were coming out of some houses and not others. The angel replied that those were prayers of believers going up to God. Those prayers were visible to my friend but even more so, they were visible to Heaven.

Our prayers impact Heaven

I used to go outside on a starry night to pray. Somehow it seemed like God could see and hear me better if there were no walls or ceilings in the way of His observation deck. When you and I pray, we sometimes feel very alone, very isolated, and very unnoticed; but the truth is, we are very much *not* alone! God gives attention to people who are faithful to pray.

Consider the story of Cornelius, a righteous man, and an Italian Roman centurion. He was praying, as was his usual pattern, when suddenly in a vision an angel appeared to him to deliver a message from God. What did Cornelius do that arrested God's attention? The angel explained to Cornelius: *"Your prayers and your alms have come up before God for a memorial before God"* (Acts 10:4 NKJV).

When I think of memorials, I think of Washington, D.C. There are memorials to presidents, to those who fought in wars, and to people who made major contributions to the United States. Those memorials were built so we don't forget significant people and events in our history. Cornelius' faithful prayers not only rated an angelic messenger, but they were established as a memorial before God to be a constant reminder to Him.

Our prayers are far-reaching

Our consistency in prayer, and even our generosity to the poor draws the attention of God. Cornelius' prayers were a direct reason His family was brought to faith in Christ the day of Peter's visit. Cornelius' angelic encounter was also a very significant event in the New Testament and even in your own life personally. You see, this was the turning point for the message of salvation to be preached to anyone not of Jewish heritage. The amazing truth is, if you are a Christian and *not* of Jewish heritage—you are a far-reaching result of Cornelius' prayers.

Our faithful prayers are powerful too and can impact our families, our churches, our neighbors, our cities, our nation, and our world. Like Cornelius, we even affect our generations yet to come when we pray.

Consider this passage written by the Apostle Peter, the very man the angel instructed Cornelius to send for in Joppa: *"For the eyes of the Lord are on the righteous, and his ears are open to their prayer."*

Amazingly, when Cornelius' men went to Joppa as instructed by the angel to find Peter, they found him—you guessed it—praying! God notices faithful prayer.

True Story: My dad served in the army at the end of World War II in Japan. During that time, he came down with pneumonia and was ultimately brought to Letterman General Hospital in San Francisco, California. My dad was a prodigal, though he had been raised to know God and had a mother who faithfully prayed for him and her other six children. Dad knew God had called him to be a pastor, but he was running from that call. Like Jonah, he had been disobedient and had chosen to go his own way. He found himself in a desperate place hanging between life and death. Outside Dad's hospital room, he overheard the doctor speaking to his mother, "If you know anyone in Texas who can pray, you should call them now. Your son will probably not live through the night." My grandmother went to prayer and so did many other family members.

Upon hearing the doctor's words, my dad turned his face to the wall and said, "God, I give up! I surrender my life to you. If you heal me, I will preach for you. But Lord, if I am going to be a preacher, I don't want to be some weak and wimpy preacher. I want the power of your Spirit operating in me in a strong and powerful way." The Lord healed my dad and fulfilled his request. God anointed him to bring people out of spiritual bondage and set captives free who were possessed and ensnared by the Enemy. Not only was my father a powerful pastor, but his voice was heard for many years on a late night radio program, "On the Road to Heaven." This program reached across our nation and into Central and South America, bringing the message of salvation to the lost. My grandmother's prayers were far-reaching, not only for my dad's life and her other six children but for all of the people who heard the gospel through my dad's preaching.

True Story: A number of years ago, the Lord began to speak to me to pray for the little girls of Bangladesh. I cannot tell you if there was an incident that brought that part of the world to my mind; I just had an inner knowing that I was to pray for the little girls of that country.

During that time, the Lord began to bring people into my path who shared more with me about Bangladesh and its culture; I prayed even more fervently. I learned how little girls there were often just an unwanted commodity.

Several years passed. One day, Bruce came to me and reminded me of some money I had been saving for missions from a part-time salary I received for overseeing the music of our church. I shared with Bruce that I wanted to use the money to help little girls in Bangladesh. He responded that we didn't know any missionaries to

Bangladesh but encouraged me to pray about it. He felt God would confirm His direction by putting someone in our path at the national ministers meeting we were soon to attend.

The opening night of the convention, missionaries from around the world were dressed in traditional clothing from the countries in which they ministered. After the service, I stood in line to pick up my children from the kids' church area. While waiting, I began chatting with the couple in front of me. They introduced themselves as Bob and Twyla McGurty, missionaries to Bangladesh!

I began to share with them my burden for the little girls of their region. They too were saddened and shared more details of the plight of little girls there. I told them of my desire to build an orphanage for girls. With troubled faces, they replied that there had been no project like it before in their country and further explained they were sure the national church would not agree to it. They felt the Bangladesh church leaders would, however, allow a boys' orphanage to be built. I responded that my money was specifically for a girls' orphanage. We agreed to pray about the matter and exchanged contact information.

In a couple of weeks, we received a follow-up call from the McGurtys. They joyfully shared the news that a missions' organization had agreed to come alongside us to partner on the project. This group would build a boys' orphanage and the national church would allow a girls' home to be built also. Today, this orphanage still stands as a testimony to the far-reaching impact of prayer from one continent to another. Children rescued by this orphanage will be able to pass the message of salvation on to their generations to come.

SOMETHING TO THINK ABOUT: God used two men who were praying, specifically, Cornelius and Peter, in order to fulfill an Old Testament scripture: "In Him shall the Gentiles trust" (Isaiah 11:10). Until that time, only the Jews had the gospel, though Jesus died to save all people (John 3:16).

Cornelius' prayers touched the heart of God thereby opening the door to the Gentiles. Peter's prayers and subsequent vision allowed God to prepare him for the task of bringing the message of salvation to the Gentiles. Both the prayer of intercession and the prayer of surrender are important and necessary to the kingdom of God. They work together to accomplish great things in order to bring many to salvation. They must be an important part of our everyday prayer journey if God is to fulfill His plan in our lives and in our world.

PRAYER EXERCISE: Pray for the Lord to give you a prayer focus for an international need. Surrender yourself to God and ask Him to open your eyes to specific details of that problem or crisis. Remember that God may use the media, your church, or the people you meet to give you direction. Be faithful to give this need a place in your daily prayers.

> *Isaiah 6:8 And I heard the voice of the Lord saying, "Whom shall I send, and who will go for us?" Then I said, "Here I am! Send me."*

Pray in Faith

2 Corinthians 5:7 For we live by faith, not by sight.

"Only God can move mountains, but faith and prayer moves God."

- E.M. Bounds

Bartimaeus had more than a loud voice that day when he cried out, "Son of David, have mercy on me!" Jesus picked him out of the multitude and healed his eyes. You might say Bartimaeus had "blind faith" and it is this kind of faith that pleases God. Faith arrests God's attention. Bartimaeus' bold request, *"Lord, I want to see,"* received an immediate response from Jesus.

Faith is a necessity if we are going to see answers to our prayers. Jesus said that faith, even tiny faith, can move mountains (Matthew 20:17). So why is it so easy to pray faithless, lifeless prayers? The Bible clearly says we can't please God, much less draw His attention, if we don't have faith. Search the Scriptures; Jesus never commended or celebrated anyone for doubting!

In Peter's courageous but unsuccessful attempt at walking on water, Jesus didn't say, "Good try, Peter! You at least got out of the boat!" When Thomas refused to believe the Lord had risen from the grave, Jesus could have said, "I understand you were going through a rough time, Thomas." Jesus didn't. He did not praise His fearful disciples, either, when they shook Him from His nap to still the storm.

In these incidents Jesus responded:

"Why are you afraid, O ye of little faith?"

"Be not faithless but believing."

"O ye of little faith, why did you doubt?"

Check the Scriptures. Fear and doubt brought a reprimand from Jesus every time. Conversely, when people acted in faith, Jesus was quick to affirm, celebrate, and applaud them:

"Your faith has made you whole."

"According to your faith so be it unto you."

"Such great faith have I not found in all of Israel!"

"O woman, great is your faith."

Faith fuels the work of Heaven. Fear and doubt are the pilot light of Hell. Faith invites, even authorizes, God's intervention. Doubt is also empowering but in reverse. **When we choose to walk in fear, we make our problem bigger than God and that is idolatry.** Remember, it was doubt and unbelief in the hearts of people that kept Jesus from doing anything of significance in Nazareth. Fear and doubt never enable any act of faith, and prayer itself is certainly an act of faith!

Many times we think that to have faith, we must have perfect circumstances. "Jesus, I could have faith if you would just..." goes through our minds. However, when Peter stepped out of the boat, Jesus didn't calm the sea for the big faith event. He calmed the storm afterwards. God did not provide Abraham with a roadmap when He called him out of Ur of the Chaldees asking him to leave home and family. It too was a faith walk and not a "cake walk." Challenging circumstances are a part of our journey from start to finish. But like Abraham, as we walk in faith, our faith will draw God's attention to us each step of the way.

Praying in faith

Here are five important things the Bible says about the necessity of faith. Notice that they defy natural logic.

The rules of faith:

1. You must believe in God (Mark 11:22; Hebrews 11:6).
2. To please God, you must have faith (Hebrews 11:6a).
3. Faith is necessary to get your prayers answered (James 1:6,7).
4. To get your prayers answered, you have to believe God will reward you for praying (Hebrews 11:1, 6b).
5. Faith in God is more important than what you see in your circumstances (2 Corinthians 5:7).

Increasing faith in our lives can feel like a daunting task. However, a faith mechanism is in us or Jesus would never have said *"Have faith in God"* (Mark 11:22). If we were not able to produce faith, Jesus would never have spoken those words, and God would certainly not be displeased with us if we were incapable of producing it (Hebrews 11:6). A farmer would never expect a marigold seed to produce a tomato if it could only produce marigolds. Faith is part of our spiritual DNA. Scripture clearly reveals we have each been given a portion of faith (Romans 12:3).

Faith is of such importance that the Apostle Paul mentioned the shield of faith as part of our spiritual armor (Ephesians 6). Paul stated, *"So then faith comes by hearing, and hearing by the word of God"* (Romans 10:17, NKJV). **We must read, memorize, meditate, listen to, and stand on God's Word in order to maintain and increase faith.** The Apostle's closing words in 2 Timothy were, "I have fought a good fight, I have finished the race, I have kept the faith." As one person said, "Paul lost his head, but he did not lose his faith."

True Story: Bruce and ten other pastors from the U.S. were visiting schools, distributing groceries, and doing outreaches in poverty stricken villages of El Salvador with the Convoy of Hope. It was communicated ahead that every mother present at the school outreaches would receive two bags of food. The school leadership provided an estimate in advance as to the number of grocery bags needed at their location, Bruce and the pastors carefully assembled the groceries the night before.

At the first outreach, more mothers arrived than had signed up. Bruce, as the Convoy of Hope representative, resolved to be true to their commitment and gave out two bags to each woman in attendance. This presented a major problem since there was no time to go back for more groceries in order to arrive at the next school on time.

Bruce and a young Salvadorian pastor were the only ones who knew of the lack of groceries. At the next outreach site, again, there were also more women in attendance than had signed up.

Before the groceries were distributed, the schools had a short service. Three of the American pastors took turns speaking through the interpreter to the schoolchildren and the mothers in attendance, as had been done at the previous school. During the meeting, Bruce and the young pastor went outside. Though Bruce did not speak Spanish and the Salvadorian pastor did not speak English, they prayed together over the food and asked God to multiply it.

When the time came to pass out groceries, Bruce and the national pastor got into the back of the truck, praying in their hearts constantly as they passed the bags of food to the U.S. pastors who were distributing them.

Miraculously, every woman received two bags of groceries. Bruce and the young pastor were thrilled for the miracle. Bruce privately wondered about the four bags of groceries still in the truck. He questioned why God would give bags of leftovers. At that moment, two little boys came running up. They explained that their mothers were sick and requested if they could bring the groceries home to them. Later, during supper that evening, the American pastors rejoiced together as Bruce shared with them the wonderful miracle God had done by multiplying the bags of food.

True Story: In 1950 my Uncle Andy, my dad's oldest brother, was injured on a construction job when a large piece of machinery fell from above, pinning him over a rail. He suffered major internal damage, and his back was so seriously injured that he was paralyzed on one side of his body. My uncle was taken to a hospital in Galveston, Texas, near where he had been working. Uncle Andy was in such terrible condition, the doctors released him as they felt they could do nothing to help him. In essence, he was sent home to die.

While being cared for at home, the only thing he could keep down was hot tea. My Uncle Andy lost from 190 pounds to 110 pounds in just a few months. Each day he dealt with constant pain. Family and friends prayed faithfully to God for him.

During this time, a healing evangelist came to Beaumont, Texas, where my uncle lived. On the last night of the revival, Uncle Andy was carried to one of the many cots surrounding the platform. During the service, the evangelist stopped in the middle of his preaching, looked at my uncle and said, "You, that was hurt on a construction job, stand and walk." At that moment, my Uncle Andy was praying for a woman with cancer lying on the cot next to him and did not hear what was said. My Uncle Bobby, who was sitting beside his brother, leaned down to get his attention. The evangelist continued to look, and said again, "You, that was hurt on a construction site, stand and walk." In that moment, faith filled my Uncle Andy's heart, and he instantly stood up and began walking! En masse, the packed house of the city auditorium stood to their feet rejoicing and praising God.

My Uncle Andy was carried into the meeting that night but left walking. After the service, he joined his family for a steak supper. From then on, my uncle was able eat anything he wanted and gained 40 pounds in two months! Uncle Andy ultimately went back to working on his construction job and later fulfilled God's call on his life to become a pastor.

SOMETHING TO THINK ABOUT: A friend of ours had a fall because of a faulty platform, which resulted in a serious injury. The same is true of our prayers. Our prayers must rest on a platform of faith in God. Fear and doubt are faulty platforms. Our faith does not rest on what we see, but in God alone. Regardless of your need or crisis, faith in the God who made the universe and brought it into orderly existence can bring your "universe" into order as well.

PRAYER EXERCISE: Hearing the Word of God increases faith, so start today to memorize a passage of scripture that counters an area of weakness or challenge in your life (i.e., fear, sickness, debt). Verbally proclaim these scriptures daily over your problems, and you will be amazed to see what God can do to build your faith through the power of His Word.

> *Mark 11:24 Therefore I tell you, whatever you ask in prayer, believe that you have received it, and it will be yours.*

> *James 1:6 But let him ask in faith, with no doubting, for the one who doubts is like a wave of the sea that is driven and tossed by the wind.*

Pray with Perseverance

Matthew 7:7,8 "Ask and it will be given to you; seek, and you will find; knock, and it will be opened to you. For everyone who asks receives, and the one who seeks finds, and to the one who knocks it will be opened."

"Prayer delights God's ear; it melts his heart, and opens his hand. God cannot deny a praying soul."

-Thomas Watson

We were driving down a major thoroughfare of our city when our 7-year-old son proclaimed, "Dad! Somebody's roof is on fire over in that new neighborhood!" Stephen continued to be so adamant that we drove a good distance out of our way to the subdivision of the burning house.

Sure enough, just as Stephen said, the roof of a house in this new neighborhood was on fire. Ironically, someone was mowing the yard next door; on the other side of the street, someone was playing basketball. All the while their neighbor's roof was on fire.

Bruce and Stephen ran to the front door, rang the doorbell and waited. No one answered. Amazingly, they could see the couple in the living room watching a football game, unmoved. Bruce rang the doorbell again several times to no avail. Finally, he and Stephen began knocking and pounding. Only then did a man come to the door, irritation etched across his face.

As Bruce explained the state of emergency, the man responded gruffly rather than in gratitude. The fire trucks arrived and began dousing the flames. Even then, this man gave no appreciation or thanks to Bruce or Stephen. All we could determine was that he could not move past what he considered a violation of polite protocol.

Earthly protocol says ring the doorbell once, maybe a second time, and then after sufficient pause, a knock or two might be acceptable. But heavenly protocol says keep on asking, keep on knocking, and keep on seeking until the answer comes. God is not annoyed at us when we ask a second, third, or a hundredth time.

As Jesus was teaching this principle of persistence in Luke 11:5-10, He told the story of a man who went to his neighbor at midnight asking for three loaves of bread. This determined man had an unexpected guest and had no food to set before him. Jesus explained that friendship alone was not enough motivation to get the neighbor to rise out of bed to respond. He said because of the petitioner's improper persistence—literally "shamelessness"—the neighbor would arise to fulfill the man's request. This word for "shamelessness" is used nowhere else in the New Testament[5] but helps us to understand the bold persistence whereby we should pursue God to fulfill our petitions.

The Syro-Phoenician woman we read about in Matthew 15, sought Jesus with this kind of audacious tenacity. Her daughter needed deliverance from demons. When Jesus put her off, she didn't get offended; she simply became more politely persistent. Our Lord marveled at her faith, honored her request, and the woman's daughter was delivered.

Persistence draws the attention of God. Jesus explained this concept in the parable of an unjust judge who honored another persistent woman's request. Luke opens up chapter 18 of his Gospel by saying, *"One day Jesus told his disciples a story to show that they should always pray and never give up" (NLT)*. Jesus said this widow badgered the judge day and night until he gave her justice. He confirmed that God actually looks favorably on us—without offense, without irritation, without saying "you're getting on my nerves"—when we persist and never give up!

True Story: My dad was a man of great persistence and faith. Though he pastored a church in a humble blue-collar area of New Orleans, he believed God could use his life in big ways. He diligently sought the Lord regularly for great things and made every effort on his part to make them happen.

My dad always had a tremendous love for Israel. His first trip to the Holy Land was only possible because he and my mother felt they should sell their only car in order to finance his travels there. Dad loved Israel so much that he went 17 times in his lifetime and encouraged others to go with him.

Prior to one particular trip, Dad really believed in his heart that the Lord wanted him to interview former Prime Minister, David Ben-Gurion, the first prime minister of Israel. My father had studied much about this powerful man who had heroically led Israel to become a nation. Mr. Ben-Gurion had been a focus of Dad's prayers for many years. My father requested for our whole church to fast and pray that God would open this miraculous door. Dad also had a few political contacts in Washington, D.C., and asked them to use their assistance and influence to accomplish this goal. Miraculously, God opened the door while Dad was in Jerusalem, and he was granted an interview.

The former prime minister really liked Dad from their very first meeting. They discussed Bible prophecy, a subject about which they were both enthusiastic and well-versed. Ben-Gurion was passionately animated as he shared how Israel had become a nation and his experiences in that process. In fact, the prime minister became so immersed in their conversation that he forgot his next appointment with a large group of teachers and unintentionally kept them waiting for two hours.

David Ben-Gurion met with my father once more on another of Dad's trips to Israel. Just a few months after Dad's second visit with the former prime minister, war broke out in Israel and prevented him from traveling there for a while. In the course of their friendship, Mr. Ben-Gurion sent my father five hand-written letters that we still treasure today. In one of them, he invited Dad to bring our family and live in his kibbutz there in Israel. A short time later, the prime minister became ill and died. My father, our family, and our church had prayed many times for Mr. Ben-Gurion. Only eternity will fully reveal the purpose and the results of those prayers.

SOMETHING TO THINK ABOUT: When I was 3 years old, I was so excited to get new shoes. My parents said I asked forty times, "Daddy, when are we going to get my new shoes?" even though we were already in the car making our way to the shoe store. My repetition did not irritate them. They were just amazed and pleased at my persistence.

When God revealed His plan to destroy Sodom, Abraham was persistent on behalf of his nephew Lot and other righteous people who would be affected. God was not offended at Abraham's powerful defense of the righteous. God responded favorably to Abraham's question— *"Shall not the judge of all the earth do what is just?"* (Genesis 18:25) —and He will respond favorably to our persistent pleas to Him also. We must not give up until the answer comes!

PRAYER EXERCISE: Is there a need that will not go away in your life? Consider a prayer jar: Put a glass jar in an area where you will see it. Every day, even multiple times a day, write prayer petitions to God asking Him to hear and answer your prayers. Include scriptures that you are standing upon. Speak your petitions aloud to God, and give thanks to Him for the answer as you drop your request in the jar. Remind God that His Word says He honors our perseverance. Ask the Lord to give attention to this prayer memorial you are building unto Him.

> *Micah 7:7 But as for me, I will look to the Lord; I will wait for the God of my salvation; my God will hear me.*
>
> *Psalm 141:2 (NIV) May my prayer be set before you like incense; may the lifting up of my hands be like the evening sacrifice.*

The Power of Praise

Psalm 34:1 I will bless the Lord at all times. His praise shall continually be in my mouth.

Hebrews 13:15 Through him then let us continually offer up a sacrifice of praise to God, that is, the fruit of lips that acknowledge his name.

"The secret of answered prayer is faith without doubt. And the secret of faith without doubt is praise...triumphant praise, continuous praise, praise that is a way of life."

-Paul Billheimer

What does a shepherd boy on an isolated hillside have in common with two men in a Philippian prison? All three caught the eye of God because of their praises to Him.

David was the youngest in a large family. He was given the seemingly insignificant job of watching his father's sheep. This lonely, isolated hillside turned out to be the very place that drew God's favor and attention because of David's continual habit of praise (Psalm 34:1, Psalm 23). The outcome was nothing short of miraculous. While David was seeking God's heart, God was seeking *"a man after my own heart,"* and He found that man in this shepherd boy, David. God had the prophet Samuel anoint him "King David."

Paul and Silas in a dark Philippian jail praised God in the midst of their newly inflicted stripes (Acts 16:24,26). How easy it would have been to operate out of human perspective and stay focused on their pain and the injustice of their situation. Paul and Silas, however, chose to disregard their circumstances and praised God in spite of their misery and mistreatment.

Their praises attracted the attention of God so that He sent an earthquake to set them free. In hindsight, we might question why God would go to such great lengths to provide an earthquake in the middle of the night, especially since city officials released Paul and Silas the very next day from prison.

Perhaps their praises so moved the heart of God that He shook the Earth, just so they didn't have to spend a terrible night in prison. Instead, Paul and Silas were treated with kindness and received food and care for their wounds. They even had a divine opportunity to share their faith in Jesus with the Philippian jailer, transforming him and his family for eternity.

Praise benefits

The Bible says God loves the praises of His people so much that He inhabits and dwells in the midst of them. When Jesus was riding in His triumphal entry into Jerusalem, the Pharisees wanted Him to rebuke those who were shouting praises. Instead, He said, *"I tell you, if these were silent, the very stones would cry out."* We are encouraged, even admonished in Scripture, to praise the Lord (Psalm 146:1,2; 9:11; 30:4; 68:4; 106:1).

Our praise blesses the heart of God, and then He blesses us in turn. Amazingly, when God requests certain things from us His children—to praise Him or to obey His commandments, for example—He always has a blessing on the other side of our obedience. The benefits that praise brings to our lives are like compounded interest: we give praise to God and He multiplies blessings back to us. Though it is never the reason we praise—we praise because God is worthy to be praised—but it is impossible not to notice the reciprocal effect praise brings to our own lives.

A praise getaway

I like to say that praise is like prayer on a vacation to outer space. I know it sounds crazy! But like a vacation, praise removes us from the everyday care, worry, and troubles of this life, which is often where most of our prayers are focused. Praise brings encouragement, rest, and tranquility to our spirits.

What about the outer space part, you might ask? The Bible is replete with God's reminders of His great power and might as reflected in the heavens. Consider that at least nine times in the book of Isaiah alone, God reminded the prophet that He is the maker of the Earth, the stars, and the universe. Those reminders helped Isaiah to see past his present difficulties to focus on the greatness and capability of the God he served. God was saying, in essence, "Look at this, not that!"

Amazingly, our planet is perfectly "suited for viewing and analyzing the universe." In fact, our planet is the only place in the galaxy discovered thus far that is a platform "for discovering the universe in its smallest and largest expressions." God purposely created our atmosphere and our position in space so we would have the perfect view of the cosmos, which displays His creative genius.[6]

Consider these amazing scriptures confirming this connection:

> *Isaiah 40:25,26 To whom then will you compare me...Lift up your eyes on high and see who created these? He who brings out their host by number, calling them all by name, by the greatness of his might and because he is great in power, not one is missing.*

> *Jeremiah 32:17 Ah Lord God! It is you who have made the heavens and the earth by your great power and by your outstretched arm! Nothing is too hard for you!*

> *Psalm 8:1 O Lord, our Lord, how majestic is your name in all the earth! You have set your glory above the heavens.*

> *Psalm 8:3,4 When I look at your heavens, the work of your fingers, the moon and the stars, which you have set in place, what is man that you are mindful of him or the son of man that you care for him.*

> *Psalm 121:2 My help comes from the Lord who made Heaven and Earth.*

When we praise God with a mindset of all He has created, we move past our planets of petition and comets of concern to the true magnitude of God. The vast 'amazingness' of countless stars, billions of galaxies, and, most of all, the immensity of our God comes into focus. Whereas, before, we could only see our little home, our church, our job, our neighborhood, now we are seeing the clear spectrum of our "pale blue dot" amid the whole of the universe. Now our impossible challenges seem not only possible but even small by comparison to God's magnitude and greatness.

Praise moves us past the pile of troubles in our own backyard to recognize the immensity of the God we serve. Praise brings our situation into divine perspective.

Let me summarize this: Praise blesses our Heavenly Father. God delights in our praises because we are His beloved children. **His Heart is blessed** and He rejoices over us. As we turn our focus toward God instead of our troubles, our hearts are lifted beyond the realms of our sufferings and trials. God's splendor and greatness surpass our earthly challenges and **our hearts are encouraged** to trust Him.

What are your worries and your burdens? Our praise must not be stifled by our circumstances. Praise Him in the midst of them. Do you have a child who is weighing your heart down or a marriage that is struggling? Praise Him in spite of your pain. Is your financial overlook a mountain of debt? God is greater! He is on the move in your situation! Give Him praise!

True Story: One Sunday morning, as I finished playing the piano at the end of the church service, I had the oddest sudden change in my vision. It was as if I was looking through broken pieces of a stained glass window. Everyone and everything around me looked fragmented and shattered.

I had seen such a thing demonstrated on the wall of my eye doctor's office where four large pictures showed what your visual field would be like if you had certain diseases.

I refused to react in fear. I said a silent prayer to God. I thanked and praised Him, believing my eyesight would soon return to normal. I went around greeting people as I usually did after a service. I even stood around and talked until everyone left. In my mind, I just kept praising the Lord that He was healing me.

As I walked into the office, I asked my daughter Bethany, "Would you please pray for me? Something is terribly wrong with my eyesight." I then described what I was seeing. As I looked through my distorted vision at her face and the face of Tuesday, my little grandbaby, fearful imaginations began to invade my mind and "What if this will be my life?" thoughts tried to rush in. I refused to give them a place because I knew God was bigger.

Bethany came over to me and prayed for God's healing for my eyes. Nothing happened, but I kept my heart in a position of faith and praised God for His healing. I took about five steps and walked into the other room. Suddenly, God totally healed me! My eyesight was instantly restored to normal.

That Sunday evening, our small group met as usual in our home. There I shared my testimony and gave praise to God. A man who had come only a couple of times to our group explained that he was presently working as an assistant to an ophthalmologist. He said the symptoms I described were very serious. He asked everyone to pray over me again so they would never return. God heard our prayers and our praises, also. Those symptoms have never reoccurred. To God be the glory!

True Story: One year we had sacrificially saved our money to vacation in Niagara Falls. It was a big trip for our family since we lived in south Louisiana at the time. Bruce did his best to make arrangements at the nicest place our budget could afford. When we arrived at our hotel, we were so disappointed. Besides the small cramped room and minimal amenities, our window overlooked a tourist attraction called, "The Criminal Hall of Fame."

No other rooms were available in the hotel. Bruce decided to make a few phone calls—all to no avail—as everything around us was booked. While Bruce continued to make phone calls, the children and I knelt by the bed and made "a call" to Heaven (Jeremiah 33:3). We asked God to do a miracle for us and then praised Him for working on our behalf. We kept our hearts filled with faith that Jesus was going to answer.

As a last resort, Bruce called a Bed and Breakfast in a nearby pricier community. Though they had no openings, the owners suggested Bruce call their friend who also owned a Bed and Breakfast. Miraculously, this next man told Bruce he had one opening. He went on to share that since their business had opened, they had never had a reservation canceled until moments prior to our call. Bruce explained to this hotel owner that this room was a direct answer to our prayers.

The new place God provided for us was such an incredible gift! It was a lovely mini hotel owned by the Bed and Breakfast next door. Each morning we ate a delicious homemade breakfast with the guests of the Inn, and then we would head into town to visit Niagara Falls, the gardens, and other attractions. In the late afternoon, we would return and enjoy the peaceful setting of our getaway in the countryside, complete with a picturesque river and a rope swing, all within our budget. We made sure to praise and thank God over and over for His many blessings. This miracle also gave us an opportunity to share our faith in Jesus with the owners of the Inn.

SOMETHING TO THINK ABOUT: Praise de-stresses us by affirming to God and to our own minds and bodies that we really believe He is working on our behalf. In the darkest dungeons of my life, in my most difficult battles, praise to God has brought relief and victory. King Jehoshaphat taught me this lesson in 2 Chronicles 20. He had a great army coming against him and the children of Israel. He sought the Lord by opening up with great praises *"to the God of Heaven"* (v.6) and ended his prayer by saying, *"We do not know what to do, but our eyes are on you"* (v.11). God responded to Jehoshaphat's request, *"Do not be dismayed...for the battle is not yours but God's."* The next day, the king went into battle sending the praise band first. As the people of Israel began to praise, God wiped out their enemies without any effort on their part. Praise is a mighty force and a powerful weapon!

PRAYER EXERCISE: Follow David's example in Psalm 119:164 and praise God seven times throughout this day. Praise Him for His mercy and His grace. Praise Him for His greatness. Praise Him for His mighty acts. Praise Him for His love and His goodness. Read Psalm 150 for inspiration. Throughout your day intersperse

58

your activities with praises to God. Step outside tonight and look at the moon and the stars that are reminders of His amazing greatness. Let the evidence of God's creativity, His provision, and His loving care birth in you a heart of praise. As a future challenge, consider making Sunday a praise day. Make it the day you turn all of your prayers into praise.

Psalm 119:164 Seven times a day I praise you for your righteous rules.

Psalm 8:12 (NLT) With all my heart I will praise you. O Lord my God. I will give glory to your name forever.

SECTION 3

HOW CAN I PRAY MORE EFFECTIVELY?

Praying in the Name of Jesus

John 20:31(NLT) But these are written so that you may continue to believe that Jesus is the Messiah, the Son of God, and that by believing in him you will have life by the power of his name.

John 14:14 If you ask me anything in my name, I will do it!

"Everything in prayer depends upon our apprehending this—In my name."

–Andrew Murray

My husband was a member of Rotary for many years. In one city where we pastored, the leaders would often request him to open the meeting in prayer. They would, however, earnestly ask him not to pray in the name of Jesus. Bruce would tell them, "I have never sought you out requesting to pray. But if you seek me out, know that I am going to pray in the name of Jesus." This went on year after year as new officers were elected to the club leadership.

The tragedy of 9/11 happened on a Tuesday, and the weekly Rotary luncheon was on Thursday. This time, those same leaders asked Bruce not only to pray but to take his time and liberty to pray as long as he desired. Bruce responded, "You know that I am going to pray in the name of Jesus." "Yes," they replied, "that is exactly what we want! Please take all the time you need!" What changed their hearts and minds? They realized Jesus is the power source to Heaven.

Why is it the name of Jesus elicits such offense today? Why do you think people here and around the world curse using the name of Jesus? It is because Hell despises His name. While curses with His name have increased, Christians using the name of Jesus in prayer have greatly decreased. Why? Because they desire not to be offensive. Many Christians are convinced it doesn't matter. What does Scripture say? Does it make a difference?

John 14:13-14 (NLT) "You can ask for anything in my name, and I will do it, *so that the Son can bring glory to the Father. Yes, ask me for anything **in my name**, and I will do it!"*

*John 15:16 (NLT) "You didn't choose me. I chose you. I appointed you to go and produce lasting fruit, so that the Father will give you whatever you ask for, **using my name**."*

There is power in the name of Jesus

Many people see themselves as wimpy Christians. They just don't realize the authority that is theirs because of the mighty name of Jesus. Here is an interesting caveat to the robbery story that I shared earlier in Day 1 to prove it:

Remember our two children Bethany and Stephen were with us in the restaurant the night of the robbery. As instructed by the robbers, we made our way to the freezer in the back of the restaurant, walking past the small closet that housed the safe. The gang leader, a gun in each hand, was crouched over the trembling manager who was struggling to get the safe open. As our 6-year-old Bethany walked past them, she said aloud, "Devil, get out of here in Jesus' name!" The gunman immediately blurted out "It's time for us to get out of here!" and began to gather things to leave. You see, even a small child has authority to use the name of Jesus! Psalm 8:2 says, *"Out of the mouth of babies and infants, you have established strength because of your foes, to still the enemy and the avenger."*

The devil wants our prayers to be powerless, puny, and pathetic. He wants us to feel embarrassed and uncomfortable in private and in public praying in the name of Jesus. Satan knows that is where the authority for miracles lies.

Healing in the name of Jesus

In Acts 3, Peter and John went to the temple and passed a man who had been lame since birth, but they left him walking, leaping, and praising God. What was the power source behind the man's healing? Peter explained that it was *"Jesus' name and the faith that comes through him that has completely healed him." (Acts 3:16,*

NIV). Both of these elements are crucial. *Our faith in Jesus* as our Savior gives us *the right to use His powerful name* for miracles as we pray.

True Story: Recently a pastor friend, Anthony Mullins, shared his miraculous story with us. Anthony was stillborn at birth. Fourteen hours after his birth, his pastor, who had been out of town, insisted on seeing him. The doctor went with Anthony's mother and the insistent pastor to the morgue in the hospital basement where Anthony's body was being kept. The doctor took Anthony out for them to see him.

The pastor laid hands on Anthony's little foot and began to command life to come into his tiny body in the name of Jesus. Anthony's childhood physician explained years later to Anthony that he watched life originate from the pastor's hand to Anthony's little baby body starting at his leg, flowing like a current around through the rest of his lifeless form. The doctor described how the pink color of life replaced the blue color of death as the healing flow circled from legs to arms, and then to his head. This doctor became a Christian as a result of witnessing Anthony's miracle.

True Story: Shortly after the terrible earthquake that happened in Haiti in 2010, a pastor friend of ours led a team into the mountains of Haiti to bring supplies to a village cut off from food and water. When the pastor and his team arrived, a voodoo priest met him at the entrance of the village and asked why the team had come. Even more, he insisted on knowing if they were Christians. The pastor tried to answer carefully since many Christians had been killed previously in that region. However, he had to be honest and share that they were Christians bringing food and supplies. The voodoo priest demanded, "Tell me about your Jesus!" This priest then explained that he had been in Port-au-Prince five years prior to the earthquake. While walking by the doors of a church, he remembered hearing someone inside say, "There is power in the name of Jesus!"

On the day of the earthquake, houses were crumbling all around this man. He could hear the people underneath the rubble crying in pain. This voodoo priest said he could see his own house swaying, just about to topple, with his wife and children inside. Immediately, the man called on the names of his gods, but none of them answered. Then he remembered the name of Jesus and the words he had heard in Port-au-Prince. In that desperate moment, he shouted, "Jesus!" Miraculously, the house instantly stabilized though the earth was still rumbling and violently shaking everything around him. The priest testified, "My gods could not save me, but your Jesus did." That day, the pastor and his team not only gave the supplies of food and water, but they shared the Bread of Heaven and the Living Water Jesus alone can give. Salvation came to the village that day because of the power in the name of Jesus.

> *Proverbs 18:10 The name of the Lord is a strong tower; The righteous run to it and are safe.*

> *Acts 4:12 And there is salvation in no one else, for there is no other name under heaven given among men by which we must be saved.*

SOMETHING TO THINK ABOUT: When we sign our name to our receipts using our credit card or our debit card, we do so based on money that is present in or credited to our account. However, Jesus gives us authority, not to operate by what is in *our* account, but by what is in *His* account. We operate from His account when we "sign" His name to our tab. If we need healing, if we need help, if we need wisdom, if we need intervention—we don't have to forge a signature. You and I have been given power and divine privilege through Jesus Christ, the name above all names!

PRAYER EXERCISE: As you take time to pray today, exalt the name of Jesus over every trial or negative circumstance that seems immovable in your life. Since every **knee** will one day bow to the name of Jesus, recognize that in a similar way, every **need** must bow to the name of Jesus. John 16: 23-24 (NLT) says, *"At that time you won't need to ask me for anything. I tell you the truth, you will ask the Father directly, and he will grant your request because you use my name. You haven't done this before. Ask, using my name, and you will receive, and you will have abundant joy."*

Philippians 2:9-11 Therefore God has highly exalted him and bestowed on him the name that is above every name, so that at the name of Jesus every knee should bow, in heaven and on earth and under the earth, and every tongue confess that Jesus Christ is Lord, to the glory of God the Father.

Pray the Word

I John 5:14,15 And this is the confidence that we have toward him, that if we ask anything according to his will he hears us. And if we know that he hears us in whatever we ask, we know that we have the requests that we have asked of him.

John 17:17 Sanctify them in the truth; your word is truth.

"There is nothing God loves more than keeping His promises...and when we stand on His word, God stands by His word. His word is His bond."

-Mark Batterson, Prayer Circles

"One way to get comfort is to plead the promises of God in prayer, show him his handwriting; God is tender of His word."

-Thomas Manton

My parents really believed the scripture, *"Man does not live by bread alone, but by every word that proceeds out of the mouth of God"* *(Matthew 4:4).* Each day on the wall in our kitchen, a verse was written on a blackboard next to our table where all seven of us shared family meals. My dad preached the Word at church and my mother helped us to memorize the Word at home.

Learning how to apply the Bible in the everyday challenges of my life was an important part of my upbringing. My dad walked me through my first major battle with the Enemy using 2 Corinthians 10:4, *"For the weapons of our warfare are not carnal but mighty in God for pulling down of strongholds."*

My mother's remedy and requirement for "meltdown moments" was to have me take my Bible and read until God gave me a "word" concerning my situation. I was so amazed each time because God really did give me an incredibly accurate answer or word of comfort in the midst of my life dilemmas from the Scriptures.

Surprisingly though, it was not until Bruce and I were pastors that I regularly began to use God's Word in prayer concerning specific situations. I had always used His Word as leverage for healing. But for other things, I believed I might be taking things out of context or misusing God's Word. I never realized how the Bible could be used in my prayer life for every need.

His Word; our leverage

Consider that lawyers regularly hire people to scour the records of previous court cases for precedents. By using those precedents in the courtroom, it gives them leverage to show that if a decision has occurred once, it should occur again. This is what God allows us to do. He encourages us to show His Word to Him as a reminder. God wants us to search His Word in order to lay hold of His promises.

George Mueller from Bristol, England, was one of the mightiest men of faith and prayer in church history. He raised over seven million dollars in today's money to support the orphans housed in his orphanages. He never once asked people for money or food. He just prayed it in. Mr. Mueller said he had never had a prayer that went unanswered. There were two important principles for using the Word in prayer that he constantly practiced.

1. He would read and then meditate on the Word of God. He said this habit enabled him to have a more meaningful and effective time of prayer.
2. He would locate a promise of God that applied to his need or situation. Placing his finger on that passage, he would plead with God to fulfill His Word on behalf of the specific need.[7]

Praying the Scriptures will transform your prayer life. John Maxwell in his book, *Partners in Prayer* shares,

"When I became serious about learning the Word of God and obeying what it taught, it made an impact on me. But when I learned to pray Scripture, that's when the Word really came alive to me. And my prayers gained new power because I was praying using God's Word, which is eternal (Ps. 119:89) ...

You will find that it changes your life. Anytime you pray God's will and His promises back to Him, you'll receive special blessings from Him."[8]

When we pray the Scriptures, rightly dividing the Word of Truth (2 Timothy 2:15), a number of things begin working to our benefit. First of all, we have the **ASSURANCE** that we are praying according to the will of God, which is important in seeing our prayers answered (1 John 5:14,15). Second, God takes notice and gives us His **ATTENTION**. The Lord told Jeremiah, *"...I am (actively) watching over My word to fulfill it"* (Jeremiah 1:9, AMP). Third, there is an **ACCELERATION** or increase to our faith, as faith comes by hearing the Word of God (Romans 10:17). Fourth, God's Word does not return void. There will be an **ACCOMPLISHMENT** of the purpose for which it was sent (Isaiah 55:11).

True Story: My summer job, after my sophomore year of college, was working at a local municipal courthouse in the New Orleans area as an intern. My boss, an assistant district attorney, was usually traveling and seldom in the office. Most of the time the only employees in our small office were his administrative assistant, myself, and another secretary—also, a summer hire.

Each day the court was in session, we would have visits from some of the courtroom employees while the judge or jury took a break. One of those employees was a court reporter, nicknamed "Cotton," an older man with a raspy voice who was rude and obnoxious. Since this was before the sexual harassment laws had been implemented, Cotton would come into our office and try to put his arms around me or the other summer intern in an effort to kiss us. The other girl seemed to be able to stand up to him without difficulty, commanding him to leave her alone. I had no experience with the like of such individuals, however, and would freeze—terrified—not knowing what to say or do. For several weeks, I walked in fear and dread of those episodes.

Finally, one day I was able to summon my courage and share with my mother what was happening at work. She hugged me and prayed with me as I wept over my frightful situation. After we prayed, Mother asked me to take some time with the

71

Lord and read my Bible in the den. She told me to ask the Lord to give me a scripture to stand on. I was still crying as I sat down in the armchair rocker. My dilemma felt hopeless, as it appeared to be a battle I would fight all summer.

I took my Bible; feeling directionless, I opened it at random. It fell open to Psalm 34. My eyes immediately landed on verse 4. *"I sought the Lord, and He answered me and delivered me from all my fears."* Shocked, I read on through a stream of tears as the next verses soothed my soul: *"Those who look to him are radiant, and their faces shall never be ashamed. This poor man cried, and the Lord heard him and saved him out of all his troubles. The angel of the Lord encamps around those who fear him, and delivers them"* (5-7). I began quietly sobbing, praising and thanking the Lord, knowing God was speaking to me and would be with me.

I stood on those verses as I went back to work the next day and every day afterward until my crisis was over. From that point on, the court reporter came back to the doorway of our office but never into the office as before. He would just stand outside and look in. It was as if there was a hedge of angelic protection that kept him out. God's Word was my two-edged sword I used to defeat the human attack of sexual harassment, as well as the Enemy's stronghold of fear in my life.

> *2 Peter 1:3, 4 (NLT) By his divine power, God has given us **everything we need** for living a godly life. We have received all of this by coming to know him, the one who called us to himself by means of his marvelous glory and excellence. And because of his glory and excellence, he has given us **great and precious promises**."*

SOMETHING TO THINK ABOUT: The greatest leverage our children have in attempting to get their way is when they say, "But Mom/Dad, you promised..." As a parent, I always tried to stand by my word, but first I made sure it really was what I said. This is what our Heavenly Father, the God who cannot lie (Titus 1:3), does when we, His children, remind Him of His promises to us and declare His Word over our situation.

PRAYER EXERCISE: As you read the Bible, the Lord will often enlighten certain passages to your heart and your life situations. Ask God to give you specific verses that would be applicable to your journey. Write these passages down in a prayer journal or wherever you can have quick access to them. Use them in prayer today and every day. Meditate on these scriptures, memorize them, personalize them, stand on them, and pray them often.

- *Psalm 119:89 (NKJV) Forever, Oh Lord, Your word is settled in Heaven.*
- *John 6:63b, ...The words that I have spoken to you are spirit and life.*
- *Psalm 119:49-50 Remember your word to your servant, in which you have made me hope. This is my comfort in my affliction, that your promise gives me life.*
- *John 15:7 If you abide in me and my words abide in you, ask what you wish, and it shall be done for you.*
- *Isaiah 55:11 So shall my word be that goes out from my mouth; it shall not return to me empty, but it shall accomplish that which I purpose, and shall succeed in the thing for which I sent it.*
- *Luke 21:33 Heaven and earth will pass away but my words will not pass away.*

Prayer Partnership

Matthew 18:19,20 "Again, I say to you, if two of you agree on earth about anything they ask, it will be done for them by my Father in heaven. For where two or three are gathered in my name, there am I among them."

"There has never been a spiritual awakening in any country or locality that did not begin in united prayer. "

- Dr. A.T. Pierson

66 **I** feel like God wants us to find a time to pray together each week for our children," announced my friend, Mindy, with a smile. I inwardly rolled my eyes at the thought of one more demand on my time. I was doing good to remember to breathe. My schedule was already full with all of the choir and worship practices, church services, and preparations for speaking, that some days I thought I would crack from the stress. "I would love to, Mindy, but I can't think of a place in my schedule where I could possibly fit in one more obligation." She persisted sweetly, "I understand. But I really believe this is from the Lord." The next week, there she was again with the same plea.

After several spurned attempts, I finally agreed to Mindy's request, cautioning her that I did not feel I could spare more than ten minutes. That has been seven years ago; Mindy and I have faithfully followed through with our prayer pact though I now live in Tennessee and she remains in Wisconsin.

Technology is a wonderful gift and has enabled me not only to pray weekly with Mindy but also to add other prayer partners on different days. Some are prayer phone calls. Some are prayer emails or texts.

The Bible tells us that there are tremendous benefits to prayer partnership based on Matthew 18:19, 20. Consider the following:

- Increased power in prayer
- Increased presence of the Lord
- Increased blessing for those who are praying
- Increased outcomes to prayer

In my prayer partnerships we briefly share our needs, and then each person takes a turn to pray for the other's requests. Praying for our nation, for Israel, and for other needs of our world are also things we try to include. I pray with some friends weekly, some monthly, and some as special needs arise.

There is one definite rule: **No gossiping!** Two of my friends were both going through a precariously difficult leadership challenge. As they shared their concerns and requests with the other, my friends moved into gossip. Within a two-week period, both of them had a tooth that abscessed on the side of the jaw where they usually held the phone. They repented to God, knowing their gossip was the cause behind the infection.

As we partner in prayer together, we are strengthened in the unity of the faith. There are many different parts of the body of Christ, according to 1 Corinthians 12, and praying together is one of the ways that the Body comes together to function more effectively. God has often drawn each person to a special focus of prayer. By praying together, we learn of new areas, needs, and topics that should be covered in prayer. As iron sharpens iron, so we, as friends and prayer partners, sharpen each other in the arena of faithfulness and effectiveness in prayer.

Prayer partnership also provides accountability and mentorship. One thing I believe God has put on my heart is to have prayer partners of different ages. My oldest prayer partner is 85 and my youngest is 7 with lots of prayer partners in between. I am committed to learning about prayer from others and teaching others what I have learned—not just in a classroom—but also by modeling prayer as Jesus did for His disciples.

Through prayer partnership, my friends and I have experienced miracles: addictions in family members broken, sicknesses healed, relationships restored, an unjust court case dropped, loved ones saved, depression lifted, marriages strengthened. The complete list of answered prayers would be too numerous to mention.

Here are a few unusual situations:

I had been sending scripture texts to my friend, Michael, though I did not know he had changed his mobile number. The new phone customer, a woman, had a son by the same name. She responded to one of my texts saying that she believed the scriptures were for her son, Michael, and asked if I would begin praying for him. Three months later, she shared that her son had come back to the Lord and had been restored to the Christian school from which he had been expelled at the time of our first correspondence.

My nurse friend, Bobbie, shared that nurses in the large city where she lived were being laid off right and left. She was concerned about losing her job, as she was within two years of retirement. We began to pray about the situation. In just a matter of weeks, her picture was on the front of one section of the newspaper, accompanied by an extensive interview with her as the runner-up for the "nurse of the year" award in that metropolitan area.

Mindy's son, Caleb, was attending a Christian university. He was suffering from fatigue and depression, very unlike him. We began to pray about the situation. Two weeks later, Caleb was miraculously voted in as the student council president to serve the following year. Just before summer, he was diagnosed with wheat and dairy allergies. He suffered from pain and lethargy if he did not maintain a strict diet. In spite of those challenges, that summer during his break, Caleb chose to travel with his school doing a mission's trip to Uganda, followed by a tour representing his university. One night at a Minnesota youth camp on the tour, God miraculously healed Caleb of his food allergies as youth pastors gathered around and prayed for him.

True Story: When we pastored in Lafayette, Louisiana, Bruce and I were impacted by a video by George O. Otis, Jr., called *Transformations*.[9] Bruce was so personally inspired, in fact, that he began gathering fellow pastors in our community to pray together. After meeting with those pastors once a month for a season of time, the pastors chose to join together along with their congregants to have collective prayer meetings to intercede for our city, our parish (county), our state, and our nation. This cohesive effort lasted for a little over a year. (Bruce and I moved a short time afterward to Wisconsin.) During that season of unified prayer in Lafayette, we as believers saw these amazing outcomes:

1. Closure of a bar and the opening of a shelter for battered women and children in the same building, refurbished, and redesigned.

2. The city council voted to eliminate all strip clubs from the city limits. A councilman, who owned one of the clubs, miraculously also voted to rid our city of them. This made the decision unanimous, putting him out of business!

3. Lafayette Parish constituents voted out legalized gambling. Amazingly, a 100-year-old horse racing track, for which our city was famous, was closed and forced to relocate.

4. Our unemployment rates (along with two other parishes that had voted out gambling) were below the national average while the rest of Louisiana was above the national average.

5. Sales tax revenues continued to climb while all other parish tax revenues decreased (indicating the consumer market was healthy).

6. Property values continued to rise while all other parish property values in our state were in a decline.

7. Crime rates went down in our city and parish.

From our vantage point, these things were all a result of the prayers of Christians praying in unity.

True Story from history: During early December 1944 of World War II, Hitler's army was trying to regain lost territory by making attacks in the front held by our tenacious Allied forces. His Axis forces were having great success cutting through our Allied lines due to the heavy rains, fogs, and swirling mists that muffled the sounds of their engines. Visibility was reduced to only a few yards. The miserable weather, which had continued since September, kept our planes grounded and our ground forces isolated.

General Patton felt very strongly that if the Allied forces were going to win the war, something had to be done about the rains. He was convinced that prayer was the only solution. Patton spoke to the Third Army chaplain, commissioning him to send out a training letter on prayer to all the chaplains: "We've got to get not only the chaplains but also every man in the Third Army to pray. We must ask God to stop these rains. These rains are that margin that holds defeat or victory. If we all pray...it will be like plugging in on a current whose source is in heaven. I believe that prayer completes that circuit. It is power."

Between December 11 and 14, a quarter of a million prayer cards and 486 training letters were distributed to our chaplains and troops. From December 16 to 19 the rains continued as our men fought bravely in spite of the lack of visibility. On the twentieth, the skies cleared, in spite of a bad weather forecast. For more than a week, our planes pounded the Axis forces to defeat and cut off all possibilities of reinforcements. When Patton saw the chaplain again in January, he said simply, "Well, Padre, our prayers worked. I knew they would." Then Patton cracked the chaplain on the side of his helmet with his riding crop to accentuate his gratitude for the chaplain's help.[10]

SOMETHING TO THINK ABOUT: Unity is a powerful factor. God confounded the human language at the Tower of Babel because they were unified in defiance (Genesis 11). The Holy Spirit filled believers on the Day of Pentecost as they were gathered in unified obedience (Acts 2). Unity can be used to empower the Kingdom of God or the kingdom of darkness. As we join together in prayer, unity will accomplish more than we ever thought possible. God loves to hear His people pray, and He loves to see them united for Heaven's purposes.

As we pray for others, we fulfill Galatians 6:2, *"Bear one another's burdens and so fulfill the law of Christ."* Prayer partnership brings encouragement to our lives. It is spiritually refreshing to have someone pray for us and for our needs. However, those prayers are more than a mutually supportive experience. Most importantly, they ascend to God in an echo. They are mighty in the heavenly realm.

PRAYER EXERCISE: Begin to pray today that God will bring you a trustworthy prayer partner with a sincere heart. Start by being faithful to pray with one person weekly until you have developed this good habit. Then begin adding other prayer partners as God leads you. Take advantage of other group prayer endeavors, such as prayer meetings or discipleship group meetings.

> *Job 42:10 And the Lord restored the fortunes of Job, when he had prayed for his friends. And the Lord gave Job twice as much as he had before.*

> *Acts 1:14 (NIV) They all joined together constantly in prayer, along with the women and Mary the mother of Jesus, and with His brothers.*

Pray the Will of God

Matthew 6:9a-10 Pray then like this: ...Your kingdom come, your will be done, on earth as it is in heaven.

"If the will of God is our will, and if He always has His way, then we always have our way also, and we reign in a perpetual kingdom. He who sides with God cannot fail to win in every encounter."

–Hannah Whitall Smith

"Spread out your petition before God, and then say, 'Thy will, not mine, be done.' The sweetest lesson I have learned in God's school is to let the Lord choose for me."

–D L. Moody

Nothing is too big for God to handle. Mathematically, it looks like this: God>my problems. The Bible is clear that "nothing is impossible" with God, and "all things are possible" with Him. In fact, it is declared four times in the Gospels, the first four books of the New Testament. The most amazing and unexpected place we find these words is in the Garden of Gethsemane: "Abba Father, all things are possible for you. Remove this cup from me" (Matthew 14:36).

This prayer seems paradoxical in retrospect of the three years of Jesus' ministry considering:

1. **He prophesied his own death** many times and in multiple ways (Matthew 12:40; 16:21; 20:17; Mark 8:31; John 2:19-22).

2. **The Old Testament prophets had already prophesied the Messiah's death** and suffering Jesus would fulfill (Isaiah 53; 52:13,14; Psalm 22; Daniel 9:5,26; Zechariah 12:10-14).

3. **Jesus prepared His disciples** for what appeared to be His final hours at the Passover supper. He had even told His betrayer, Judas, to do what he must do.

81

On one hand, Jesus appeared to be fully aware of and fully committed to the plan of His Father. Yet, minutes later, in the Garden of Gethsemane, He prayed, *"Abba, Father, all things are possible for you. Remove this cup from me: Yet not what I will, but what you will"* (Mark 14:36). Even after all these self-prophecies, the prophecies of old, the preparation of His disciples—Jesus still knew all things were possible with God—even in the last hour. He knew personally His situation was not beyond His Father's control.

What are you facing, which seems too big for God to answer? Is it your marriage, your family, your finances, or your health? Remember, nothing is impossible with God. But also remember God knows the end from the beginning. He knows what is the best outcome. He knows what is the best timing.

Consider a lesson from King Hezekiah's life in 2 Kings, chapter 20. King Hezekiah was sick unto death. God sent His prophet, Isaiah, to tell the king to get his house in order; he would not recover from his illness. Hezekiah cried out to God, reminding the Lord of his faithfulness during his reign as king. God honored his prayer and sent Isaiah back to tell Hezekiah that He would heal him and give Hezekiah fifteen more years. However, the king didn't realize God's initial plan was in his and his descendants' best interest. Within three years of Hezekiah's extended life, he had a son named Manasseh who became possibly the most wicked king to have ever reigned in Judah. During those fifteen extra years, Hezekiah also made the terrible mistake of showing all of the royal treasures and storehouses to envoys from the king of Babylon. The tragic result of Hezekiah's disclosure was that his descendants were later taken into captivity in Babylon, as prophesied by Isaiah. It was an exile, which lasted for 70 years and included the physical ruin of Jerusalem. In our humanity, we, like Hezekiah, can only see things from our earthly perspective and often make our requests to God from that vantage point.

The Apostle Paul's "thorn in the flesh" is a mystery none of us fully understand. Paul said he prayed three times for the Father to remove it. The Lord's response was, *"My grace is sufficient for you, for my power is made perfect in weakness."* Paul did not get bitter or angry at God's reply as some of us might have done. Paul's response was: *"Therefore I will boast all the more gladly of my weaknesses, so that the power of Christ may rest upon me. For the sake of Christ, then, I am content with weaknesses, insults, hardships, persecutions, and calamities. For when I am weak, then I am strong"* (2 Corinthians 12:8-10).

When we pray, we must believe God has our best interest at heart. Jesus had to trust His Father's plan was "for good and not for evil," (Jeremiah 29:11; Genesis 50:20) even when the suffering that lay ahead did not *look good* to Jesus. "Now we know in part" (1 Corinthians 13:12), and we must trust God, who knows all things, by praying for His will to be done, even while we pray in faith for our miracle.

True Story: The Lord spoke to Bruce in prayer that our church was to buy property and relocate. He gave Bruce the exact amount of $300,000 we were to spend. Property prices were very expensive in the area of the city in which Bruce felt led that our church was to build. In spite of this fact, we found a beautiful piece of property of 36 acres. The problem was, we had no money. Here are the miracles God did:

There were 57 owners of the property. The predominant owner was a wealthy lady with controlling interest. She personally shared with Bruce at the closing how she had heard an audible voice in the middle of the night, hours before our church proposed a bid on the property. The Voice said she would receive a bid the next day and she was to take it, along with the conditions requested. (i.e., Our request was that we would assume ownership of the property with no exchange of money, and we would pay the full $300,000 within the year, with no interest.)

The miracle of prayer behind the story: Her neighbors—a single mom, Mary, and her teenage son, Shane—attended our church. They faithfully prayed for this lady every night asking the Lord to use her for His Kingdom. There were many times this mother and son got up in the middle of the night and prayed for their neighbor. God answered their prayers.

In spite of those miracles, we had such difficulty in getting sufficient funds for the payment of that property. We prayed in faith, but we also prayed the will of God be done. It was grieving our souls knowing that we had received such a miracle but could not come through with the money. We had made a commitment not to borrow any funds. We were $32,000 short of our goal the evening before the money was required to be in the bank. As before, we prayed fervently for a miracle, but we also said, "Your will be done, O Lord."

The next day, an hour before Bruce was required to make the deposit at the bank, a businessman from our church, unaware of the deadline, felt a great urgency from the Lord. He turned around on his trip to Houston and brought the $32,000 to the office of the church. His original intent was to give the money the following Sunday. God performed a miracle with not a moment to spare.

True Story: My beautiful and talented sister-in-law, Polly, struggled with an aggressive brain tumor for a little over 2 years. She and my brother, Chip, were pastors and Christian music artists, well-known across the nation for their singing duo. Polly, Chip, and their two sons fought bravely to save her life. Family members and hundreds of friends sought the Lord faithfully for her. We earnestly prayed in faith for Polly's healing, but as we could see the great toll the cancer was taking on her, we also prayed the will of God be done. Two months before Polly's heavenly home-going, she saw a vision of Jesus, angels, my parents, and her dad, who had gone on six months before, in Heaven. She spoke with awe and wonder as she tried to describe to my brother, Chip, the beautiful things she saw.

It has been very hard to understand God's plan in taking Polly home. We, her family, greatly miss her. However, we have been strengthened in knowing that God knows the end from the beginning and that His ways are higher than our ways. We are comforted that Heaven awaits!

SOMETHING TO THINK ABOUT: Each one of us has prayer crossroads. There are times that we have pushed and pulled, desperately trying to get answers for our difficult situations. Praying for God's will to be done is not a sign of a lack of faith or of *giving up*; it is a sign of *giving in* to what God knows is best.

The cross certainly didn't seem like the best choice to Jesus in the Garden of Gethsemane. However, because of our Savior's submission, provision for salvation was made for all who will call upon His name. As we continue to earnestly seek the face of God for our answers, we can trust His decisions.

PRAYER EXERCISE: You may be facing a hard decision today with a lot at stake. If you are wondering whether you should be praying the will of God or the prayer of faith over your difficult situation, do as Jesus did: First, have faith for the impossible! Proclaim the promises of God's Word over your situation. Second, stand in faith, and pray your desired outcome. Tell God what you would like for Him to do. Third, pray for His perfect will to supersede your own will. When that is done, trust Him. Leave it in His hands, and live in peace, believing for God's will to be done.

> *Matthew 6:33 But seek first the kingdom of God and his righteousness, and all these things will be added to you.*

Pray with Recall

Psalm 103:2 Bless the Lord, O my soul, and forget not all His benefits.

Psalm 145:5,6 (NLT) I will meditate on your majestic, glorious splendor and your wonderful miracles. Your awe-inspiring deeds will be on every tongue; I will proclaim your greatness.

"Christian, remember the goodness of God in the frost of adversity."

-Charles Spurgeon

My daughter, Bethany, and I were reminiscing about Christmases past. I said, "Remember when 'such and such' happened?" She didn't. I ventured further... "You know, it was the year Aunt Joy had the fish fry." She still didn't. "You know, it was the year when so and so threw away the gravy." Suddenly the light came on, "Oh, you mean the year Grannynu gave all of us cousins teddy bear jog outfits!" We both had a good laugh. We realized I catalog memories by food, and she catalogs memories by fashion.

It only stands to reason, one of my favorite miracles in the New Testament is a story about food. Jesus multiplied one little boy's small lunch to feed 5,000, plus.

Let's think about the disciples for a moment as they were on the inside tract of this miracle.

1. They saw the need and even asked Jesus to send the multitude away.

2. They helped to find part of the solution—the little boy with the "happy" meal.

3. They witnessed the miracle, helped to serve the crowd, and even saw the abundant twelve basketfuls left over.

That was in Matthew, chapter 14. Now fast forward just a little to chapter 15, and here they were faced again with the same dilemma. This time, the crowd was a little smaller. Did their experience with the 5,000 provide a platform of faith for Jesus to perform a similar miracle for the 4,000? Not on your life! They were just as faithless as before.

Now rewind to the Old Testament book of Exodus. Israel was at the point of being able to enter the land God promised them. When they saw the giants amidst the beauty and the abundance, did they remember how God had parted the Red Sea for them? Did they remember how God fed them manna every day? Did they remember the water He provided in the desert? ...the voice that thundered from Heaven? ...the cloud that led them by day or the pillar of fire by night? No! No! No! Their faith account was bankrupt (Psalm 106:7-13).

Why is it, even after great miracles, we see the same faithless behavior in both Old and New Testaments? I believe it is because those people chose to erase their memories like a repossessed computer. They so easily forgot what God had done for them.

One day while I was thinking about those strange, faithless responses, the Lord spoke to me and said, "This is exactly how you respond when a great challenge arises in your life. You act like I have never done anything for you or answered any of your prayers in the past. You act hopeless as if I will not help you." I repented to the Lord and realized how faithless I had been time after time.

How easy it is to forget God's faithfulness. Without making a special effort to remember, we too will be like those who have gone before us. We must purposely write down the things God has done for us, and remember His answers to our prayers. We must look at those miracles regularly, and use them as platforms of faith for future miracles. We must share them with others to increase their faith, also. The enemy stands ready to erase our memories and our faith.

True Story: My parents were scheduled for a trip to Singapore. Two weeks before their trip, my mother fell and broke her elbow, right at the joint. Dad took her to the emergency room where they did x-rays. The doctor decided to wait until the next day to put her arm in a cast because of the swelling. Naturally, Mother was quite frustrated about her injury. Besides the pain and misery, it looked like the trip to Singapore would be impossible.

The next day, to add aggravation to injury, after laboriously loading her dishwasher one-handed (as her other arm was in a sling), my mother's dishwasher quit working. She later told me how she got so mad at the Enemy, she laid her hand on the dishwasher and said, "Devil, I rebuke you in Jesus' name! Leave my dishwasher alone!" Right then, the dishwasher began working!

The incident so filled my mother's heart with faith; she touched her broken arm and rebuked the devil again, proclaiming her arm healed in Jesus' name. The pain immediately vanished. Removing her arm out of the sling, she began praising the Lord, moving her arm back and forth and up and down with complete mobility. Mother was totally healed, to the amazement of her doctor. She never had another moment of pain! She went on her trip to Singapore two weeks later, praising God, and testifying to people of her miracle all along the way!

True Story: Marie Segura is a special friend and mentor in my life. She was my mother's prayer partner for 20 plus years until my mother went to Heaven. Now at 85, Marie and I are prayer partners. She has prayed for me and my family almost since the day she met us. (Her daughter Polly married my brother, Chip.)

About 40 years ago, Marie had almost completely lost her vision due to an incurable eye disease that doctors said would leave her totally blind. They gave her no hope of recovery. However, shortly after she became a Christian, God intervened miraculously during a church service. Today, though Marie has no side vision, she is able to see clearly with "tunnel vision." She has testified of God's healing miracle in her life to many people and on many occasions.

This last year she had her first eye exam in years. The doctor proclaimed in utter amazement, "You are a total miracle! With everything I see from your exam, you should be completely blind!" Marie shared with her doctor the wonderful testimony of God's healing intervention for her eyes.

Because of this miracle, Marie has been able to see her children and her grandchildren grow up. Now, she is enjoying her great-grandchildren. She can still watch TV and even read.

Shortly after her salvation, Marie was called by God to be a prayer intercessor, teacher, and mentor. She believes God restored her vision in this way so she would stay focused on the prayer ministry to which He has called her. She has prayed faithfully for so many people and has testimonies of great miracles God has done. One of my favorite answers to prayer through Marie's prayer partnership was meeting my husband, Bruce. She has continued to pray for Bruce, our children, and me all of these years.

SOMETHING TO THINK ABOUT: How well do you remember? It is true we are not to depend on sight in order to have faith. However, when God gives us "sight" or evidence He is working, and we choose to not remember, it displeases Him.

What are you doing to actively remember God's faithfulness? I find it helpful to keep a book of remembrance, journaling the things God has done in answer to my prayers. As I log in each blessing along my way, it provides layers of strength upon which to build my faith for other petitions yet to be answered. I also try to share my testimonies with others to build up their faith. God is pleased when He sees our efforts to remember His goodness and faithfulness to us.

PRAYER EXERCISE: Make a special place in your prayer journal for recording God's answers to your prayers. Here are some categories to help trigger your memory: salvation, protection, provision, problems solved, addictions broken, healing miracles, and divine recoveries. Develop an ongoing habit of thanking God daily for the many ways He has intervened in your life.

Psalm 77:11, 12 I will remember the deeds of the Lord, yes, I will remember your wonders of old. I will consider all your works and meditate on all your mighty deeds.

Psalm 145:4 (NLT) Let each generation tell its children of your mighty acts; let them proclaim your power.

Pray in the Spirit

Ephesians 6:18 Praying at all times in the Spirit, with all prayer and supplication. To that end keep alert with all perseverance, making supplication for all the saints.

Ephesians 5:18 Do not get drunk with wine, for that is debauchery, but be filled with the Spirit.

"The Holy Spirit does not do all the work for us in prayer but works with us! It is a joint effort. As we depend on God's Spirit in prayer, He will show us how and what to claim in prayer."

- Dick Eastman

We had just finished Sunday lunch at our home in New Orleans. Normally, Sunday afternoon was rest time in my parents' home. However, at the age of 11, I knew something was different. My mother went to her room, not for a nap, but to pray. We could all feel the heaviness of heart as my mother prayed in her room. We kids prayed too as we worked to finish the dishes. Mother felt so strongly that something was wrong with my oldest sister, Ruth, who was a freshman at a college in Texas.

Mother was crying out to God, praying in the Spirit for more than an hour, when we received a call from Ruth. She and several of her friends had been involved in a car accident as they were returning from church. They were all rattled but safe. We knew God had protected them in answer to my mother's prayers and ours' too. Though Mother did not know what or how to pray, the Holy Spirit helped her.

In the Spirit

Many people believe "praying in the spirit" means to pray more fervently or even to pray as directed by the Spirit of God for special things or specific directions. Although both of those things are true, they do not give the complete biblical meaning of praying "in the Spirit."

The Apostle Paul said in 1 Corinthians 14:18, *"I thank God that I speak in tongues more than all of you."* He made it clear that it was not in the church that he did this. So when was it? It was in his time of prayer and intercession. Notice his instructions in Ephesians 6:18, *"Praying always with all prayer and supplication in the Spirit...for all the saints."* Even Paul, who was an excellent wordsmith, did not have enough words to accomplish this feat without the empowerment of praying in the Spirit. He addressed the matter of praying in the Spirit, specifically praying in tongues, in 1 Corinthians 14:14,15 (NLT):

> *"For if I pray in tongues, my spirit is praying, but I don't understand what I am saying, well then, what shall I do? I will pray in the spirit, and I will also pray in words I understand. I will sing in the spirit, and I will also sing in words I understand."*

There are four things in this passage which confirm praying *"in the spirit"* is praying in tongues:

1. Paul says that when you are *"praying in the spirit,"* you don't understand what you are saying. It would be impossible for a sane person to be praying and not understand what they are saying unless Paul was referring to speaking in tongues.

2. Paul says that when you *"pray in the spirit,"* your spirit is praying (see also 1 Corinthians 14:2). Notice that to *"pray in words I understand"* involves the mind rather than the spirit.

3. The phrases, *"pray in tongues"* and *"pray in the spirit,"* are used interchangeably in this passage and are shown here to have the same meaning.

4. Paul reiterates this comparison three times collectively in verses 14 and 15, his final argument being singing *"in the spirit"* (i.e., in words I do not understand) as differentiated by singing *"in words I understand."*

The benefits

The Bible also specifically shows there are benefits of praying in the Spirit. The first benefit is when we don't know exactly how or what to pray, the Spirit of God will pray through us, as previously mentioned in the story of my mother's prayers for Ruth. As we pray in the Spirit, we don't have the worry of wondering what to pray for or whether we are praying according to the will of God. The Spirit of God, who knows the will of God, the mind of God, and the details of the situations hidden from us, makes intercession for us according to the will of God. Then God, who knows what is the mind of the Spirit, responds to our prayers (Romans 8:26, 27).

The second benefit of praying in the Spirit is the renewing and refreshing it brings for our own spirit (1 Corinthians 14:4, Jude 20, and Ephesians 3:16). Praying in the Spirit builds up our faith and strengthens us. Encouragement and strength are needed in every believer's life.

True Story: At times my mother would feel impressed to pray and cry out to God, knowing only it was for someone in need. During those times she would pray in the Spirit and would also pray any details she felt prompted to pray with her understanding.

One day during a time of prayer intercession, she reminded God of her faithfulness. She said, "Lord, I have tried to be faithful to you by praying when your Spirit has prompted me. Most of the time, I have not known the reason or the conclusion. Could you, just this time, show me for whom I am praying?" The Lord showed my mother a vision of a little girl crying in a very dark place. My mother wept and cried out to God in the child's behalf until the burden lifted.

That night as my mother watched the news, there was an amazing story of a little girl who had been rescued by two hunters earlier that day. Walking past an old abandoned house in the woods, these two men heard the cries of a child coming from an outhouse nearby. There they discovered a little girl placed in the sewage by an evil person who had abducted her. Though the child's picture was not shown, the news program revealed the exact description of the little girl my mother had seen in her vision.

True Story: Bruce and I have felt impressed by a sense of urgency and warning to pray in the Spirit on many occasions in our times of travel. On one such event, we were returning from Houston to our home in Louisiana. There were seven of us in a van—three adults and four teenagers. Bruce and I simultaneously felt an urgency to pray. We asked everyone to join us by praying in the Spirit. Minutes later, we were in the middle of an eleven-car accident. Cars in front of us and cars behind us collided into one another. One car even ended up partially on top of another. Our car and one other car in the middle were the only ones that escaped— undamaged. We knew God had heard our prayers!

True Story: The Haitian voodoo priest who came to faith in Christ (see Day 10) went down the mountain after the pass was reopened to the pastor's church. He wanted to be water baptized as the pastor who led him to Christ had instructed him.

It was such an important occasion to all of this man's friends and family that most of the village made the journey to witness his baptism. This new believer had only been taught the message of salvation and the need for water baptism. The pastor had never given any instructions or information about the baptism of the Holy Spirit because of the short time he and the rescuers had been in the village.

As the former voodoo priest was submerged into the baptismal waters, his village friends looked on intently. Their curiosity turned to amazement when he came up speaking in a language he had never learned. At that moment, every villager lined up, unprompted, to be baptized as well. As each of these new believers was baptized, they also came up out of the water speaking in tongues.

SOMETHING TO THINK ABOUT: During a visit to Haiti, Bruce posed a question to one of the national pastors: "How many churches in Haiti would be considered Spirit-filled?" The national pastor responded that regardless of the denominational affiliation of the churches, they were *ALL* Spirit-filled. He went on to explain how no church could survive without the power and boldness, which comes with the baptism of the Holy Spirit, because of the intense spiritual warfare that exists in Haiti. Should you and I desire anything less, considering the challenges we face in our world? If you and I are to fulfill the great work of God's Kingdom on this Earth, we must have the Holy Spirit's empowerment.

PRAYER EXERCISE: *John 16:13a says, "When the Spirit of truth comes, he will guide you into all the truth."* If this chapter has brought questions to you, go on to the next chapter and simply pray today for the Holy Spirit to guide you into the truth of God's will in this matter. Take time to read the book of Acts on your journey of truth. (If you desire to learn more about this subject, please refer to the Appendix.)

On the other hand, if you desire this special gift from God, pray today to receive the infilling of the Holy Spirit. Even if you are unsure of what praying in the Spirit looks like, trust God for this gift. He hears our prayers and will respond to your yearning heart.

If you have already been filled with the Spirit, use this special gift to be more effective in your prayer life. Consider new places (e.g., your car, your shower, your closet) where you can devote yourself to this privilege of praying in the Spirit. You can also pray anytime throughout your day as Ephesians 6:18 says, *"Pray in the Spirit at all times and on every occasion. Stay alert and be persistent in your prayers for all believers everywhere."*

> *1 Corinthians 14:2 For one who speaks in a tongue speaks not to men but to God; for no one understands him, but he utters mysteries in the Spirit.*

Prayer with Fasting

Ezra 8:21,23 Then I proclaimed a fast there at the river Ahava, that we might humble ourselves before our God, to seek from him a safe journey for ourselves, our children, and all our goods. So we fasted and implored our God for this, and he listened to our entreaty.

"Fasting is like a hidden truth that has been forgotten or purposely misplaced and ignored by the Body of Christ over the last century. Yet I have found that fasting is one of the greatest weapons that God has given to His end-time army!"

-Mahesh Chavda, The Hidden Power of Prayer and Fasting

Prayer and fasting go together in the Bible much like salt and pepper do on our dinner tables. Each is a complement to the other. Fasting, like prayer, draws us closer to the heart of God and our fasting draws God's heart closer to us.

Many Christians think fasting is only for a few spiritually zealous, high achievers. However, Jesus made it clear that we, His disciples, would not only pray (Matthew 6:5-7) but we would fast as well: "When you fast," says Mark 6:16,17.

Fasting was a big issue with the Pharisees and scribes, the religious watchdogs of Jesus' day. They asked Jesus why His disciples did not fast as did John's disciples. Jesus responded, *"As long as they have the bridegroom with them, they cannot fast. The day will come when the bridegroom is taken away from them, and then they will fast in that day"(Mark 2:19, 20).* You and I live "in that day" to which our Lord referred.

Jesus Himself fasted, setting an example for us. He fasted 40 days before His temptation by Satan in the wilderness, just before the launch of His public ministry. In our human thinking, if we were going to face Satan, the tempter of tempters, we would not want to leave ourselves physically vulnerable by going without food. The Spirit of God, however, purposely led Jesus directly into the wilderness, knowing our Lord would have the spiritual strength necessary for the battle that lay ahead—only if He fasted.

Biblical fasting is more than not eating or limiting the kinds of food we eat during a specific timeframe. It is setting aside a greater space for God in our daily agenda. Fasting is making a choice to humble ourselves before God. It is a time of surrendering our will to His Will. Biblical fasting requires us to get rid of wrong mindsets, motives, and behaviors as we repent and wholeheartedly turn to God. It empowers us to forgive, mend fences, and move forward toward Christlikeness. When done properly, fasting changes the way we pray, the way we live, and the way we treat others (see Isaiah 58:3-12).

Fasting also brings supernatural help from Heaven. Consider some instances of individual and corporate fasting recorded in the Bible that brought divine intervention and spiritual transformation:

- Queen Esther and Israel humbled themselves through fasting and prayer. God intervened by protecting Esther as she went before the king and by preserving the people of Israel from annihilation (Esther, chapters 4,5,8,9).
- King Jehoshaphat and Israel humbled themselves through fasting and prayer. God preserved Israel by wiping out their enemies who far outnumbered them (2 Chronicles, chapter 20).
- Ezra and Israel humbled themselves through fasting and prayer. They had no defending forces to protect them on their return to Jerusalem after the Babylonian captivity. God granted them safety on a very dangerous journey (Ezra, chapter 8).
- Nineveh, a rebellious Gentile nation, humbled themselves through fasting and prayer. God relented from destroying them as was His original plan spoken through the prophet Jonah (Jonah, chapter 3).
- Daniel the prophet humbled himself through fasting and prayer. God sent an angel with a message in answer to his prayers (Daniel, chapter 9).
- King Ahab, a notoriously wicked king of Israel, humbled himself through fasting. God chose not to bring the destruction He had promised to Israel in

100

Ahab's lifetime (1Kings 21:27-29).

- Believers in the upper room fasted and prayed. God sent His Holy Spirit to baptize and empower them on the Day of Pentecost. It is a gift that keeps on giving (Acts, chapter 2).

- Cornelius fasted and prayed and an angel was sent with a message to him. As instructed by the angel, Peter was summoned. He preached the message of salvation to Cornelius and his family, opening the door of salvation to the Gentiles (Acts, chapter 10).

Lessons learned from failure

Jesus taught His disciples two important concepts when they failed to cast the demon out of the desperate father's son (Mark 9:17-29, NKJV). Jesus first admonished them that faith is not only important; it is mandatory. Second, He shared that victory for certain difficult things requires prayer and fasting. We must recognize this humanly distasteful addition to prayer is a means by which we can see the hand of God move in the resistant situations of our lives. Fasting is like a booster rocket to our prayers. It brings spiritual steel to our faith and an amplification of God's anointing for accomplishing His work on this earth.

True Story: When we were pastoring in Lake Charles, the Lord put it upon Bruce's heart to go on a three-day fast. We have often looked back and laughed because instead of losing weight, Bruce gained five pounds during those three days. As we recently re-examined our time of ministry there, however, we were amazed at two supernatural things that took place, notably after that fast:

First miracle: A cheerleader in our local high school was in a terrible accident. She was a neighbor of one of our church members who asked Bruce to go to the hospital to pray. When Bruce arrived at the hospital, he did not realize the doctor had already signed the girl's death certificate. The mother of the child angrily tolerated Bruce to pray for her (already deceased) daughter. As he prayed, God miraculously healed the teenage girl, restoring her smashed face, her broken body, and her life in a matter of seconds.

The second miracle involved a young man who had been in a bar room brawl. Someone in the community had called the church and asked Bruce to go and pray for "Tony." When Bruce arrived at the hospital, Tony was being kept alive by machines. There were no brain waves; his body was on life support for the purpose of organ donation. The hospital staff allowed Bruce to go and pray for the young man. He quietly moved to Tony's bedside and leaned down close to his ear. Bruce introduced himself and then began to speak to Tony about the condition of his soul. My Husband asked Tony to repeat the sinner's prayer in his heart as he himself prayed aloud. Bruce continued praying past that prayer of salvation and asked God to heal Tony. As he turned to leave, Bruce heard the voice of the Lord say, "He is going to live." In spite of the doctor's outrage, Tony's family chose not to unplug him from life support as a result of the words God had spoken to Bruce.

Miraculously, within the next four to five weeks, God restored Tony's brainwaves, brought him out of a coma, and began to restore his ability to talk and walk. Shortly afterward, Tony was transferred to a hospital in Houston for rehabilitation. Bruce, however, was not informed of Tony's move due to confidentiality laws and felt disturbed since he did not know of Tony's welfare. Without knowing the name of any family member or even the person who had initially made the call, Bruce had to leave the matter in God's hands.

Weeks later, while we were visiting a church member in a Houston hospital, Bruce and Tony divinely reconnected in a hospital hallway. As Bruce greeted a nurse, Tony, who was walking by, recognized his voice, stopped and said, "Hey, you're Pastor Bruce!" Tony thanked my husband for saving his life by courageously sharing the word of the Lord to his family and standing strong in spite of the doctor's curses at his bedside. Most importantly, Tony thanked Bruce for praying with him in his brain-dead condition. He said he had heard, understood, and prayed along with Bruce to receive salvation in those desperate moments between life and death.

True Story: When our daughter Bethany was about 10 years old, she began to have problems with her ankles. Some days, even weeks, she would go to school using crutches because it hurt to walk. Though perhaps unrelated, during this time she also began to have numbness, which started at her feet and began moving up her legs. I made an appointment with Bethany's doctor since the symptoms were not going away. With great concern and heaviness in my heart, I decided to fast and pray at the church. I located myself in the choir room overlooking the recreation area where Bethany had lunch and physical education at our church school. Feeling desperate for a miracle, I cried out to God all through the day for Bethany's healing.

When Bethany got out of school in the afternoon, I asked if she was still having problems with her legs. She first shared with me how the numbness had come up to the middle of her thighs that morning. Then she smiled and told me how, in the afternoon, the symptoms completely disappeared. We praised the Lord together believing God had healed her. Since we still had the appointment, Bethany and I hurried on to get to the doctor's office in time. As we met with her physician, Bethany shared her symptoms of the recent days and weeks. The doctor responded with visible relief as Bethany related to her that the numbness was completely gone. The physician then explained how those symptoms could indicate a very serious illness and should they ever reappear, we were to call her right away. (I know now those symptoms can indicate multiple sclerosis.) Bethany never had the numbness return again and the problem with her ankles also cleared up shortly thereafter.

SOMETHING TO THINK ABOUT: Fasting is difficult for most of us to do. It affects our daily patterns, our social routine, and our culinary pleasures. It impacts our physical strength and our emotional buoyancy. How can we be obedient to God's call to fast when the challenges are—so challenging? Here are two things that will help:

1.We must remember though the difficulties are great, the rewards are much greater. Consider 2 Corinthians 4:16-18: *"So we do not lose heart. Though our outer self is wasting away, our inner self is being renewed day by day. For this light momentary affliction is preparing for us an eternal weight of glory* *beyond all comparison, as we look not to the things that are seen but to the things that are unseen. For the things that are seen are transient, but the things that are unseen are eternal."*

2. Jesus will be on hand to help us. One of the temptations Satan used against Jesus at the end of those forty days in the wilderness was the challenge to turn stones into bread. Satan knew Jesus was more than capable of this miracle, and he also knew Jesus was very hungry (Luke 4:2). Hunger was a very real issue even for the Son of God, or the Enemy would never have used that ploy. Because Jesus has faced hunger during a fast, He can help you and me when we are dealing with the same. Hebrews 2:18 says, *"For because he himself has suffered when tempted, he is able to help those who are being tempted."*

PRAYER EXERCISE: Begin to pray today for the Lord to show you how to follow Him in the discipline of fasting. Prepare yourself; learn more by reading what the Bible has to say on this subject. Listen to sermons. Read books and articles that will inspire you.

Start small by setting aside one meal to humble yourself to fast, and to pray. From that day forward, commit to growing in your endeavors. Make a list of things you are asking from the Lord before you fast. Afterward, make a list of the answers God brings as a result of your fast. It will bring encouragement and inspire you to fast in the future. Seek the Lord to give you grace, wisdom, and direction for this new spiritual endeavor.

> *Matthew 6:16-18 And when you fast, do not look gloomy like the hypocrites...But when you fast, anoint your head and wash your face, that your fasting may not be seen by others but by your Father who is in secret. And your Father who sees in secret will reward you.*

> *Romans 8:18 For I consider that the sufferings of this present time are not worth comparing with the glory that is to be revealed in us.*

Section 4

HOW CAN I ERADICATE HINDERANCES TO MY PRAYERS?

Prayer Snags

Psalm 139:23,24 (NLT) Search me, O God, and know my heart; test me and know my anxious thoughts. Point out anything in me that offends you, and lead me along the path of everlasting life.

"I firmly believe a great many prayers are not answered because we are not willing to forgive someone."

-D.L. Moody

"If the Christian does not allow prayer to drive sin out of his life, sin will drive prayer out of his life. Like light and darkness, the two cannot dwell together."

-M.E. Andross

There is nothing more frustrating and ineffective than a car that won't start. You turn the key, but all you get is a miserable whining sound from the engine—worse yet, no sound—only a dead click. This is how we feel when we pray but it seems we are making no headway with God.

When our car isn't moving, we know it's time to check the gages on our dashboard. Is there any gas in the vehicle? Is the battery working? Is there any oil in the engine? I am not a mechanic, but I know that much. The Bible also gives us some spiritual maintenance we must do in order to keep our prayers from being dead and ineffective. Through the rest of this chapter, let me walk you through some obstacles that hinder our prayers:

Vain repetitions

Matthew 6:7 (NLT) When you pray, don't babble on and on as people of other religions do. They think their prayers are answered merely by repeating their words again and again.

Vain repetitions are not to be part of our prayer repertoire according to Matthew 6:7. Does this mean we should not pray written prayers or prayer requests from a list we use each day? No. Jesus didn't say repetition is bad. He said mindless, repetitious verbalizations are unacceptable to God—not sincere, heartfelt prayers.

Sin

Psalm 66:18 (NKJV) If I regard iniquity in my heart, the Lord will not hear.

Scripture shows sin separates us from God (Isaiah 59:2). It separated Israel. It separated King Saul. It separated David, and it will separate us, also. Jesus said not to give any place to the devil (Ephesians 4:27), and this is exactly what sin does. There is a divine solution: Repentance, which is confession to God and forsaking our sin (Psalm 51; 1 John 1:9,10).

In the Lord's Prayer, as recorded in Matthew 6:9-13, Jesus taught us to repent of our sins: *"Forgive us our trespasses"* (12). Perhaps the Lord wanted our personal need for forgiveness to be a *daily prayer* since it is linked to our petition for *daily bread.*

Wrong motives: James 4:2-3(NLT) speaks very strongly that wrong behaviors, motives, and attitudes can devastate our prayer effectiveness: *"You want what you don't have, so you scheme and kill to get it. You are jealous of what others have, but you can't get it, so you fight and wage war to take it away from them. Yet you don't have what you want because you don't ask God for it. And even when you ask, you don't get it because your motives are all wrong—you want only what will give you pleasure."* Wrong motives are a dead-end street when it comes to prayer.

Relationship issues

Relationship issues can hurt our prayers in a big way. The Bible lists three that are a major hindrance.

1. Refusal to forgive others: Jesus deals very strongly with the subject of forgiving others in at least three places. Do you know where those places are? Interestingly, they are all connected to passages on prayer.

- **The Lord's Prayer**

    The first is a contingency clause within the Lord's Prayer: *"Forgive us...as we forgive,"* which connects to the nearby verse, *"For if you forgive others their trespasses, your heavenly Father will also forgive you, but **if you do not forgive others their trespasses, neither will you Father forgive your trespasses*** (Matthew 6:12,14,15).

- **Mountain moving prayers**

    The second prayer/forgiveness connection immediately follows the Lord's teaching about prayers that move mountains: *"And whenever you stand praying, if you have anything against anyone, forgive him, that your Father in heaven may also forgive you your trespasses. **But if you do not forgive, neither will your Father in heaven forgive your trespasses*** (Mark 11:21,25,26, NKJV).

- **Binding, loosing, and the prayer of agreement**

    The third prayer passage linked to forgiveness concerns the power we have to bind and loose in prayer and the prayer of agreement (Matthew 18:18,19,20). Immediately following these teachings on prayer, Jesus continued with an unforgettable response to Peter's question about the frequency of forgiving offenders (v.21). Here, Jesus shared the parable of the ungrateful servant, underscoring the absolute necessity of forgiveness: *"And in anger his master delivered him to the jailers, until he should pay all his debt. So also my heavenly Father will do to every one of you, if you do not forgive your brother from your heart"* (Matthew 18:34,35).

You have probably heard it said, "Punishing another person by refusing to forgive them is like drinking poison and waiting for the other person to die." The poison of unforgiveness will destroy you, your relationships, and negatively affect your generations to come. It keeps God's forgiveness from you. It will ruin both the earthly and the eternal plans God has for you. And, yes, it will hinder your prayers!

2. **Honor:** The Bible speaks specifically to men about honoring their wives and its effect on their prayers. 1 Peter 3:7 (NLT) says, *"In the same way, you husbands must give honor to your wives. Treat your wife with understanding as you live together. She may be weaker than you are, but she is your equal partner in God's gift of new life. Treat her as you should so your prayers will not be hindered."*

The Word of God shows we are to treat *everyone,* including our spouse, with honor and respect (1 Peter 2:17). In fact, the Bible lists many specific groups of individuals we are to honor. I call it "the circle of honor."

As pastors, when Bruce and I did marital or family counseling, it would always be evident when a part of the circle was out of balance. Dishonor is like a warped tire. One area of dishonor can hinder progress, even stop an entire vehicle, so to speak, whether it is in a marriage, a family, a school, a church, or even a nation.

Consider some areas of honor the Bible specifically addresses:

- We are to honor God (Revelation 4:10,11).
- Husbands and wives are to love, honor, and respect each other (1 Peter 3:7; Ephesians 5:33).
- Children are to honor their parents (Exodus 20:12; Mark 7:10; Ephesians 6:2).
- Parents are to give a kind of honor by showing kindness and love to their children, not provoking them. This includes not abusing them physically, spiritually, emotionally, or mentally (Ephesians 6:4; Colossians 3:21; Ephesians 4:32).
- Church leaders are to receive honor from those they are leading in the faith (1Timothy 5:17; Hebrews 13:7,17).
- Governmental authorities are to be shown honor by us as Christians (Romans 13:1-5; 1 Peter 2:17).
- Everyone is to be treated with respect, which is an aspect of honor (1 Peter 2:17).

- Our lives are to be a display of honor in everything we do (1 Peter 2:12; Hebrews 13:18; Colossians 3:17).

When we show kindness and honor, even to those we consider least in our lives, we do it as unto the Lord (Matthew 25: 37-40). When we open the door of dishonor to those that God has put in our lives, we grieve the Spirit of God, and our prayers are hindered. God takes the subject of honor very seriously (Leviticus 20:9; 2 Kings 2:23,24; Acts 23:3-5).

3. Unresolved differences. The Bible is clear, if there is an unsettled issue with our brother, we are to try to resolve that difference before offering our sacrifice: *"So, if you are offering your gift at the altar and there remember that your brother has something against you, leave your gift there before the altar and go. First be reconciled to your brother, and then come and offer your gift"* (Matthew 5:23,24). According to Jesus, it doesn't matter whether we feel we are not at fault or whether we think the other person is at fault. The issue here is to remove offenses from another person's path that would keep them from following the Lord. This is the bigger picture.

Many people have stopped serving God because another Christian offended them. Sadly, the stumbling block affects not only their life but can impact their entire family's decision to follow the Lord, sometimes for generations to come. It is not worth such a travesty. God cares so much about this issue that He says you are not to pray until you have cleared this up.

Prayer is a form of sacrifice to God (Psalm 141:2; Hebrews 13:15). In these situations, we must do what we can do. However, we cannot change another person's heart if they refuse to acknowledge our sincere endeavor of reconciliation. Romans 12:18 says, *"If possible, **so far as it depends on you**, live peaceably with all."*

True Story: My friend Iris was miraculously healed of deafness the moment she received Jesus as her Savior. All of her family came to Christ through the miracle, except her father. The family prayed year after year for his salvation.

Iris and her sister, though they each had made a decision to follow Christ, resented each other and got along very poorly. There were things each could not forgive concerning the other. One day, they realized that their father was nearing the end. The fact that he had not become a Christian weighed heavy on their hearts. Realizing they must do all they could to help their dad, they came together and repented to each other and to God. They forgave one another and put their differences aside so that they could pray in unity for their dad's salvation.

Within two weeks of their reconciliation, Iris's father made a decision to receive Jesus and become a believer. He told his daughters, "I knew God had to be real if He could cause the two of you to resolve your differences and love each other."

SOMETHING TO THINK ABOUT: Have you ever wondered if some teachers purposely give tests to see how many students they can fail? Some of my teachers in high school and college would brag about how few students could make an A in their class. God is not like that. He desires all of us, His children, to succeed. (Read God's interaction with Cain in Genesis 4:3-7 as proof.) Just as our earthly teachers rewarded us for following their instructions, the same is true of our Heavenly Father. If we desire to receive answers to our prayers, we must take seriously our responsibility to do what God requires. The ball is in our court.

PRAYER EXERCISE: Pray today that the Lord will reveal any sins in your life, any offenses with others that need to be addressed, or any persons you have not forgiven. Repent, release these people to God, and let them go. Ask the Lord to show you how to honor others and to repair any relationship that needs mending. Continue to make these matters a high priority of prayer until you have done everything within your power to live in peace with others. Commit to a daily pattern of following God's plan in your relationships.

> *Ephesians 4:31,32 Let all bitterness and wrath and anger and clamor and slander be put away from you, along with all malice. Be kind to one another, tenderhearted, forgiving one another, as God in Christ forgave you.*

The Things that Matter

John 4:23 But the hour is coming, and is now here, when the true worshipers will worship the Father in spirit and truth, for the Father is seeking such people to worship him.

"It is not the body's posture, but the heart's attitude that counts when we pray."
"Remember that you can pray anytime, anywhere...and know God hears."

– Billy Graham

Position, place, and time have all been areas that Satan has used to torment me in my prayer life: "You didn't pray on your knees. You didn't pray in your prayer closet today. You didn't pray long enough." I decided to put his accusations to rest by countering with scripture passages and the big picture of the Word, just as Jesus did when He was tempted in the wilderness.

Finding the position and place

Growing up, I believed to be holy, *really holy*, I had to be in a certain position or place to pray for my prayers to really count to God. For instance, the Bible mentions praying on our knees (Psalm 95:6; Luke 22:40-41) and lifting up holy hands (I Timothy 2:8; Psalm 134:2). I regularly follow those patterns because I believe God mentions them in His Word for a reason. The Bible also mentions praying in our prayer closet (Matthew 6:6) and praying in a corporate setting with other believers (Matthew 21:13; Acts 2:46; Hebrews 10:25). These are certainly important places and positions of prayer, however, they are not the only ones, and we should not be limited by them.

We sometimes get hung up on the designated places only to miss the undesignated ones. Prayer closets are good, church is great, lifting up holy hands is awesome (unless you are driving), praying with your eyes closed—well most definitely *not* if you are driving!

My friend, Ann, was praying during her drive time one day. She confessed to me later that she got inspired in her praying and distracted in her driving. "I went through a four way stop and hit another car!" she moaned. I responded, halfway teasing, "But Ann, don't you remember what Jesus said? He said to 'WATCH and pray!'"

Location, location, location

Hezekiah prayed in his bed. Jesus prayed in the wilderness. Daniel prayed in the lions' den. Elijah prayed for fire to come down. The three Hebrew children prayed for no fire but went through the fiery furnace victoriously. God heard all of those prayers, but none of them were kneeling, in a closet, or with hands lifted.

God hears our prayers wherever, whenever, and however we call upon Him. If we are going to go beyond our present prayer status, we must also think outside the box and pray on our knees and on our skis, at the job or eating corn on the cob, at the mall or playing ball, at the stove or at the cove, in the car or traveling afar. At the risk of sounding like a Dr. Seuss book, the point is— any place is a prayer place.

Shallow or deep

The Bible shares the prayers of many people. From the elementary prayer of the repentant sinner in Luke 18:13 to the deep, personal prayer of Jesus in John 17, we see God hears both simple and profound kinds of prayers. Wherever you are on your prayer journey, the most important thing is just to begin the journey. Don't let your lack of ability or experience stop you from praying. **Just pray!**

The long and the short of it

Does it matter if our prayers are short or long? Jabez, seemingly a nobody in scripture, prayed a short prayer to God. Now generations later, as we pray those same words, we can still experience the overflow of blessing that came his way in answer to his prayer (1 Chronicles 4:10).

On the other hand, Daniel prayed long prayers of confession and intercession for his nation (Daniel 9). Daniel's prayers brought angelic intervention and prophetic insights that have impacted generations. They have provided inspiration and patterns for us to pray for our own nation.

By Jesus' own example, there is a time and a place for both long and short prayers. The Lord's Prayer is short (Matthew 6:9-13). Christ's personal prayer (John 17) is long, giving evidence that both are acceptable to God.

To speak or not to speak

We know God hears all of our prayers whether audible or silent. David definitely favored praying aloud as do most of the references in the Bible in regards to prayer. David said, *"O Lord, in the morning you hear my voice"* (Psalm 5:3a). Psalm 18:6 says, *"In my distress I called upon the Lord; to my God I cried for help. From his temple he heard my voice, and my cry to him reached his ears."*

There are evidences that God hears silent prayers, too, or else Paul would never have instructed us to pray "without ceasing." Our vocal chords could never sustain unceasing vocalizations. Also, how could we go about all day praying aloud in the marketplace of life? In many venues, it would simply bring a reproach rather than be a witness.

Abraham's servant prayed in his heart and received an immediate answer from God (Genesis 24:45). Hannah prayed silently in her heart with only her lips moving and God heard (1 Samuel 1:10-20). Whether you pray aloud, silently, or somewhere in-between, God is listening and answering. Isaiah 65:24 says, *"Before they call I will answer; while they are yet speaking I will hear."*

True Story: Granny and Granddaddy Horton, my husband's maternal grandparents, were praying people. They had pastored many years in rural communities and lived out their remaining days in a small farmhouse in central Alabama.

We were attending Granddaddy Horton's funeral when a man and his wife walked up to Bruce and his brother, Gregg. "You must be Bruce," the man said, to which Bruce extended his hand of welcome. "Your wife's name is Marsha, your daughter's name is Bethany, and your son's name is Stephen. You pastor in Lafayette, Louisiana." Bruce responded in the affirmative as the man turned his attention to

Gregg. "And you must be Gregg. Your wife's name is Joy; your sons are Adam and Nathan. You pastor in Dallas." Gregg and Bruce both looked a bit puzzled, as they had never met the couple before.

"We were your grandparents' neighbors across the holler," the man continued. "Every night we could hear your grandparents praying for all of their children and grandchildren by name. With their windows down, their voices carried right to our home. Many nights we would just sit on our front porch and listen." Moved with emotion, the man shared, "One night, your grandparents prayed for us and said, 'Father, we don't know if our neighbors have committed their lives to serving you. If they haven't, would you save them, dear Lord?'" The neighbor shared how both he and his wife got out of their rocking chairs, knelt down on the porch and prayed to receive Jesus. The man concluded, "We came to salvation that night through your grandparents' prayers."

SOMETHING TO THINK ABOUT: Recently a teacher of a men's Bible study asked me, "How can I get the men in my class to pray aloud? It is like pulling teeth," he said. I suggested he teach a study on the many prayers in the Bible prayed aloud by men. I encouraged this man to share with his students what is at stake—our spoken prayers help teach our children and grandchildren how to pray by our example. As we pray aloud, we can release blessings over our children and grandchildren that will impact their futures and that they will long remember (e.g., Jacob over his sons). I will never forget the pleasure I felt as a child just hearing my mother and father pray aloud for me, even at times when they did not know I was present and listening.

Through the years, most of my own devotional prayers have been silent. More recently, however, I have found a great comfort in praying aloud. I believe that audible praying does at least two things that are superior to silent prayers: 1) Praying aloud helps us to keep our focus, and 2) hearing our audible petitions brings a source of comfort and strength to our hearts. There is something about hearing our own voices cry out to God that gives rise to faith, assuring us that God is hearing our cries and answering our prayers.

PRAYER EXERCISE: As you pray today, make it a point to vocalize some of your prayers aloud. Plan to do this every day, even if in the beginning you have to write your prayers and then speak them. This method will help to rid you of some of your inhibitions about praying aloud. Remember, when you pray audibly you have a greater chance to pass along your faith. Praying aloud also brings others into prayer partnership with you, multiplying your prayer effectiveness. God wants us to be comfortable in prayer whether we are praying silently or aloud.

> *Psalm 3:4, I cried aloud to the Lord, and he answered me from his holy hill.*
> *Psalm 104:34 May my meditation be pleasing to Him for I rejoice in the Lord.*

SECTION 5

HOW CAN I INCREASE THE FREQUENCY OF MY PRAYERS?

Keep on Praying

Jeremiah 33:3 Call to me and I will answer you and will tell you great and hidden things that you have not known.

I Thessalonians 5:17 Pray without ceasing.

"There is not in the world a kind of life more sweet and delightful than that of a continual conversation with God."

-Brother Lawrence

I always get amused on an airplane when the flight attendant begins to give instructions: "In the unlikely event of an emergency and the occurrence of a loss of cabin pressure...pull down on the mask to start the flow of oxygen... and breathe normally." Are you kidding? When you are falling from the sky breathing through an extended straw to stay alive— "breathe normally"?!!!

God wants prayer to be as automatic as breathing, regardless of the state of emergency. He wants prayer to be such a part of us that regardless of what is going on, we "breathe normally." Needs come in. Prayers go out. Blessings come in. Praise goes out. Breathing is to the body what prayer is to the spirit.

The Apostle Paul's life exemplified this concept. He endured many trials, faced lions, was stoned and left for dead, was whipped and beaten, was mistreated and misunderstood. In the midst of it all, though, he seemed to come very close to living out his own instruction to believers to "pray without ceasing." Andrew Murray, in his classic book on prayer said of Paul,

> "A study of Paul as a pattern of prayer will bring a rich reward of instruction and encouragement. The word our Lord used of him at his conversion, 'Behold he prayeth,' may be taken as the keynote of his life. The heavenly vision which brought him to his knees ever after ruled his life."[11]

121

The Apostle Paul traveled throughout the Roman Empire spreading the Gospel. He lived much of his life on the go. During his travels and times of imprisonment, he wrote fourteen books that comprise one-third of the New Testament and wrote other writings that were not preserved to our present day. He lived a full life. Yet, he mentioned his habits of prayer, frequency of prayer, and specific prayers he prayed for the people in the churches to whom he wrote, at least fifteen times. Consider a few of them:

> *Romans 1:9,10 "For God is my witness...that without ceasing I make mention of you always in my prayers."*

> *Ephesians 1:16 "I do not cease to give thanks for you, remembering you in my prayers."*

> *1 Thessalonians 1:2 "We give thanks to God always for all of you, constantly mentioning you in our prayers."*

> *2 Timothy 1:3 "I thank God whom I serve...as I remember you constantly in my prayers night and day."*

In order to follow Paul's example, we must make purposeful decisions to incorporate prayer into our lives in new ways. A constant attitude and aptitude of prayer do not come naturally to us as Christians. It must be developed. Therefore, we must become creative and determined in our efforts.

New ways to pray more

Each day of our lives, thoughts process constantly through our brains. Sometimes there are huge spaces of time where we fill our minds with other people's ideas and opinions. Television, Internet, and music are just a few of those ways. You and I have authority over the space between our two ears. No one can make you think or believe his or her thoughts unless you choose to do so.

Prayer is a way of bringing your thoughts captive unto the obedience of Christ (2 Corinthians 10:4). It is also a way to make your thoughts count by turning them into prayer petitions in order to make a difference eternally. The following are some ways I have attempted to increase the flow of prayer in my own life:

- **Prayer stations**

  One of the ways the Lord has helped me to increase my prayer life is through what I call "prayer stations." These are certain strategic places and locations in which I find myself every day. My bed, my bathroom sink, my shower, my kitchen, and my car are all places I try to use as prayer stations.

  Sometimes, I have certain topics of prayer for each one. At other times, those places just serve as a reminder for me to pray what is on my heart. In several of those areas, I have placed scriptures that inspire me to pray.

- **Prayer workouts**

  There are also exercises or stretches that can lend themselves to prayer. My favorite is one I learned from a chiropractor friend. Its greatest physical benefit is to help keep the body in alignment. By adding prayer, however, it also helps keep the spirit in alignment. (This Prayer Alignment Stretch is described in the Appendix at the end of the book.)

- **Prayer activities**

  Prayer activities are another way to increase time with God. Prayer walks are a favorite of mine and can be done alone or with another person. When walking with a friend, you can take turns praying back and forth for each other's needs, for your families, for your neighborhood or community, for a specific region, or for world issues at large. By the time you have finished, you are refreshed spiritually and physically.

True Story: We were in Japan for a ministry opportunity and one of the local Christians shared an amazing testimony with us. In the city of Tokyo, there had been reoccurring incidents of suicide along the tracks of one of several transit lines that ran throughout the city. This specific train line was the only one in the city not requiring family members to pay for damages and lost time due to the suicide incident. Christians in the area were naturally troubled by the terrible tragedies. They banded together and began to do prayer walks alongside the railway tracks. God heard their prayers and the incidents were supernaturally reduced.

SOMETHING TO THINK ABOUT: Before missionaries are sent to new fields where the gospel has not yet reached, strong believers are often dispatched ahead to do prayer walks. These preparatory endeavors have enabled the work of God's Kingdom to be established more effectively in those regions. We have personally seen God close businesses that were perversions in our community through consistent prayer endeavors. Would you consider taking a prayer walk or a prayer drive in the neighborhoods of your city? God will give strategies and ideas to reach the lives of those around you as you seek His Face.

PRAYER EXERCISE: Choose one or more of the strategies for increasing prayer in this chapter: prayer stations, prayer workouts, or prayer activities. Begin to incorporate them into your personal daily routine or weekly schedule. As you see an increase in effectiveness and commitment in your prayer life, share it with a friend. Consider doing a prayer walk with your spouse, neighborhood friend, or church group.

> *Nehemiah 1:6 Let your ear be attentive and your eyes open, to hear the prayer of your servant that I now pray before you day and night..."*

Recognize Prayer Opportunities

Colossians 4:2-4(NLT) Devote yourselves to prayer with an alert mind and a thankful heart. Pray for us, too, that God will give us many opportunities to speak about his mysterious plan concerning Christ.

"There is no wonder more supernatural and divine in the life of a believer than the mystery and ministry of prayer...the hand of the child touching the arm of the Father and moving the wheel of the universe."

-A.B. Simpson

My parents were pastors—excellent pastors. One day as we were riding in the car, I overheard their discussion to each other about a ministry challenge in their lives. My dad expressed how after each service he had so many people who shared their prayer requests with him; he was overwhelmed trying to remember them all. My mother echoed his sentiments, adding that if someone's condition deteriorated, or worse yet, they died, she felt terrible if she had forgotten to pray about the need.

My parents made a decision right there. If anyone asked them to pray, they would pray with that person about their need on the spot. Their decision made them even better pastors.

Don't delay. Pray.

Their conversation changed the way I do prayer. It brought prayer out of the prayer closet and into the moment, whether I was in the church or in the marketplace. Try it yourself and see how amazing it is! When you have a need that arises in your life, don't stop to think about it, just pray. When a person gives you a prayer request, discreetly pray with them right then and there. It may surprise them, especially if you are out in public, but prayer is worth the awkward moment. We have many people who have shared testimonies of how God answered those simple, on-the-spot prayers.

125

True Story: My mother-in-law, Jimmie Ruth, was ironing clothes one hot summer afternoon. Bruce was about 18 months old and was on the other side of the room playing. He was wearing only a diaper since they did not have air conditioning. The iron was on "cotton," the hottest setting. Jimmie Ruth turned to hang up a newly pressed shirt. In that instant, baby Bruce raced from the other side of the room and hit the ironing board. The impact caused the iron to fall off the board onto his inner thigh. His mother could hear his skin sizzle as the iron hit, and Bruce instantly began screaming. As she raced to his rescue, Jimmie Ruth cried out to God for His intervention. Miraculously, as she lifted the iron, there was not any redness, burn, or injury.

True Story: One day, Bruce was at the checkout counter of the grocery store and asked the cashier how she was doing. "Terrible," she replied. "My husband just left me for a younger woman." My husband asked if she would allow him to pray for her. She hesitated, then said in a half whisper, "You mean right here? Now?" Bruce told her he was sure that those in line wouldn't mind waiting for a moment. Turning to the customers behind him, Bruce asked for their permission. With surprised looks, they nodded in the affirmative. Turning back to the lady, he asked how she wanted him to pray. "I want my husband back," she responded. Bruce prayed and then finished checking out. He assured this lady he would continue to pray about the matter.

A couple of weeks went by, and Bruce was in the woman's line again. She shared with him that her husband was now depressed because the younger woman had left. Bruce again prayed for the restoration of this cashier's marriage.

Each time Bruce returned, he learned an update, gave a word of encouragement, and prayed with this cashier. One day, the woman shared that her husband was miserable and wanted to come back home. Bruce advised her that she and her husband should go to a Christian counselor first. He then prayed with her before leaving. The cashier accepted and followed Bruce's advice. After weeks of counseling, this woman's marriage was restored.

Turn thoughts into prayers

I have learned when a person comes to your mind, consider that God put them there, and pray for them. My friend, Margaret, came to my mind one day out of the blue as I was washing dishes. I prayed for her as I continued my work. A couple of hours later she called me and said, "I had the most severe headache today." She went on, "But the strangest thing happened—all of a sudden, it just completely went away!" I shared with her the time of my prayer for her, and the time of her healing coincided perfectly! We praised the Lord together, knowing it was God's prompting and His healing power that accomplished the work!

This pattern of a thought followed by an inner prompting to pray, is the guidance of the Holy Spirit. Sometimes, I have not even personally known the person I have felt impressed to pray for. At times, it has been a public figure or an entertainer. I have tried to be faithful, as the Lord has confirmed to me at times through news reports, that it indeed was His leading to pray.

Take prayer into the marketplace

When the lame man was healed in front of the Beautiful Gate (Acts chapter 3), it caused quite a stir in Jerusalem. Why? I believe it was because his healing occurred in a public place. Though miracles were done through the hands of the apostles prior to this incident, those miracles had occurred only in private settings or in the temple (Acts 2:42-46). When miracles began to happen in the public arena, more people were added to the church (Acts 5:12-16).

As Bruce and I go through our day, we try to follow the disciples' example of taking Jesus into the marketplace. At the restaurants where we eat, we leave a salvation tract (with at least a 20% tip). We also ask our waitress/waiter (our hotel clerk, the convenience store cashier, or whomever God puts in our path), if there is a need about which we can be praying. Prayer is something everyone needs, and most people don't refuse, even if they don't go to church or have a relationship with God.

Recently when we asked our waiter if he had a need about which we could be praying, he requested us to pray for his little boy to be safe and protected. A short time later, when he returned to our table, this waiter disclosed that he was an atheist. We were amazed that this man was willing to share his request since he did not believe in God. It is my opinion that in the heart of every person there is an awareness of God, whether or not the individual has acknowledged Him. Prayer gives the Lord a chance to reveal Himself even to people who doubt Him or His existence.

We have had some incredible things happen. In one restaurant, our waitress knelt at our table and prayed to receive Christ. On another occasion in a local deli, we saw a friend who was a local university soccer player. She had a sports injury and was with her teammates where we were lunching. As we prayed for her there, God healed her right in front of her soccer team!

Other things have taken longer before hearing the answer, as with Steven, our waiter at a steakhouse. His car was giving him major problems and he had just received a costly estimate at an automotive place. After we prayed with him, Steven decided to have his father's friend check it out. This older man liked to tinker on cars and discovered that the problem was actually a bolt that had fallen off. This friend had the exact bolt in his garage that Steven needed on his car. It was a real testimony of God's love and care to our waiter.

We will never know the final outcomes of most of our encounters until we get to Heaven because of our constant travels. But it has been amazing to see how many waiters and waitresses remember us when we do have a chance to return. Just recently, we had a waitress in New Orleans who came to our table to thank us for praying for her son. He had been incarcerated at the time of our visit weeks before, and she was thrilled to report that her son was out of jail and doing very well.

God wants us to bring His presence and power with us everywhere we go. We are called to be salt and light, making a difference in the world around us. Prayer is an entry point that often opens the door for people to meet Jesus and to experience His love and power.

True Story: During our season of ministry in Wisconsin, we had a series of connected encounters. Since our two children attended a high school that was about 25 minutes from the church and 25 minutes from our home, we covered a good bit of territory in the course of a day. We would eat from a varied list of restaurants in very different locations.

One day we asked our first-time waitress, Natomi, about her needs and told her about our prayer ministry. She hesitantly opened up and shared that she really needed some new shoes for her work as her old ones were falling apart and becoming hazardous. After praying with her, we really felt, along with our tip, we should personally give her the money for those shoes. She seemed touched by our kindness. We also invited Natomi to our church. She was surprised because it was the kind of church for which she had been searching.

A couple of weeks later, we were in a totally different part of the Milwaukee area. When we asked our new waitress about prayer, she suddenly became excited. She was sure we had been her roommate Natomi's customers at a restaurant in another part of town a few weeks earlier. We fit the description and details her friend had shared. This time, we prayed for Sierra, feeling an assurance in our hearts that God was up to something.

More weeks later, someone gave our family tickets to a Brewers baseball game with passes to the specialty restaurant within the ballpark. Our family was enjoying the fun occasion when our waitress walked up. She was so stunned to see us! It was Sierra whom we had met a few weeks before, miles away! We were all excited and amazed that our paths had once again crossed, now at her second job in this exclusive stadium restaurant.

When Sierra got home that night, she, Natomi, and their other waitress roommate, Stephanie, began discussing the evidence that God must want them to attend our church. We were so happy when they all three came. God did an amazing work of restoration and discipleship in all three of those beautiful girls.

Natomi and Stephanie, both talented singers, ultimately served in our worship ministry. Sierra became one of our most remarkable teachers for little ones. Today they are all serving the Lord in different parts of the country. We have stayed connected and refer to them as our "daughters in the Lord." We are still awed at the miracle hand of God and how He brought us all together through prayer and divine guidance.

SOMETHING TO THINK ABOUT: God's plan is to order our steps so our lives make the greatest impact on the world around us. When we are intentional about our daily opportunities, we find there are more spaces to use prayer as a vehicle for sharing Christ in our hurting world. Forming new habits of prayer is worth the effort as we see more answers and more miracles in the lives of those God places in our paths.

PRAYER EXERCISE: Ask the Lord to make you mindful of the prayer opportunities He has prepared for you today. Stay alert to words and thoughts given by God, and take opportunities to speak to the people He has placed in your path. At the end of your day, make a list of the people and the needs about which you should continue to pray in your prayer journal. List any supernatural details that occur to help inspire you to be faithful to this divine endeavor in the future.

> *Jeremiah 10:23 I know, O Lord, that the way of man is not in himself, that it is not in man who walks to direct his steps.*

> *Psalm 25:12 Who is the man who fears the Lord? Him will he instruct in the way that he should choose.*

> *Proverbs 3:5,6 (NKJV) Trust in the Lord with all your heart, And lean not on your own understanding; In all your ways acknowledge Him, And He shall direct your paths.*

SECTION 6

HOW CAN I INCREASE THE SCOPE AND CIRCUMFERENCE OF MY PRAYERS?

Growing in My Ability to Pray

Luke 11:1 Now Jesus was praying in a certain place, and when he finished, one of his disciples said to him, "Lord, teach us to pray, as John taught his disciples."

"Learning to pray is like learning a trade. We are apprentices and must serve time at it. Consistent care, thought, practice and time are needed to become a skillful prayer."

–Dick Eastman

My little granddaughter, Tuesday, prayed the most eloquent prayer one day when she was 4. I said, "Tuesday! Where did you learn to pray so beautifully?" She tilted her head, looked at me in a funny way and responded, "From you, Lovey! You're a praying world!" That brought tears to my eyes and joy to my heart. Tuesday had heard me pray on the phone with my prayer partners, listened to my numerous prayers for her, and she and I had prayed together many times.

Growing up in a pastor's home, I was also mentored in prayer by listening to my parents pray. Based on my experience, I believe one of the best ways we can grow in prayer is to pray those things we hear other godly people praying. The realm of our present acquaintances or mentors should not limit us, though. There are many books and websites that record prayers for specific needs. There are great preachers whose prayers have been recorded, such as Charles Spurgeon or D. L. Moody. We can also learn prayer patterns from great praying men of history like George Mueller, Brother Lawrence, or "Praying (John) Hyde."

The Bible gives us tremendous helps to improve our prayer effectiveness by learning from the prayers of the writers of the Old and New Testaments and, most importantly, our Lord Jesus. The Lord's Prayer or "The Our Father," as some refer to it, is a powerful prayer we should pray regularly. It is a form of prayer mentorship since Jesus taught it in response to His disciples' request, *"LORD TEACH US TO PRAY."* It is a great prayer for the beginner but is an important framework of prayer for the experienced intercessor. Consider the following important foundations that are condensed within this most important prayer:

1. Render to God the praise He deserves. *"Our Father who art in Heaven. Hallowed be thy Name."*

2. Realign your will to God's will. *"Thy Kingdom come. Thy will be done on Earth as it is in Heaven."*

3. Request God's provision daily. *"Give us this day our daily bread."*

4. Repent of your sins. *"Forgive us our trespasses..."*

5. Release offenses and forgive the wrongs of others. *"...as we forgive those who trespass against us."*

6. Request God's guidance and His help to avoid evil. *"Lead us not into temptation but deliver us from evil."*

7. Recognize and declare God's power and authority in your life and in your world. *"For thine is the Kingdom and the Power and the Glory forever amen."*

Consider some other aspects of prayer we can learn from Jesus as He prayed for others: *"Father, I do not ask that you take them out of the world, but that you will keep them from the evil one"* (John 17:15). He also prayed, *"Simon, I have prayed for you that your faith may not fail and when you have turned again, strengthen your brothers"* (Luke 22:32). We can use both of these examples to pray for our loved ones, even those who, like Peter, have made mistakes that need mending.

The psalmist David wrote many prayers in the book of Psalms that are also a guide in praise, deeper dedication, and repentance (Psalm 51; Psalm 19:12,13, 14; Psalm 139:23,24). David prayed a beautiful prayer on behalf of his generations to come in 2 Samuel 7:18-29, requesting that they be blessed and be established before the Lord. It is a reminder that we can be bold before God in asking for our children and our future generations to serve the Lord and find favor and blessing in His sight.

The Apostle Paul gave us wonderful examples of things he prayed for his friends in the different churches he established. Those prayers and instructions help us in developing new and effective ways to pray for our family and friends in their spiritual growth (Philippians 1:9-11; Ephesians 1:16-19; 3:16-19; Colossians 1:9,10; Colossians 2:6-8; Philippians 2:15; Ephesians 5:15).

Mentorship is a powerful tool for growth. As you study the prayers of Daniel, Hezekiah, Jehoshaphat, Nehemiah, Ezra, and many other godly men and women of the Bible, it will inspire you to remember that each of those prayers brought amazing responses from God. They were written so you and I could also learn how to pray prayers that move the heart and hand of God.

True Story: The summer before we married, Bruce was serving as youth pastor at my dad's church in New Orleans. One Sunday night, we were returning with some of our youth group from a ministry event we had conducted in another church across town. As we drove past our local church, it was evident something unusual was happening—lights were on in the building and cars were still in the parking lot—though it was past 10 p.m.

After stopping to check out the situation, Bruce shared with me that my dad needed him to remain and for me to go on home. That night, along with other praying men, Bruce supported my dad in prayer as a man was delivered from demonic possession. It was an important night of prayer mentorship in Bruce's life. Just a little over a year later while we were serving on a short-term missions' assignment to Alaska, God used Bruce to pray the prayer of deliverance for a man who was bound by the powers of darkness. The important prayer mentorship Bruce received from my dad that night in New Orleans was a very significant factor in Bruce's boldness to pray for the man's deliverance in Alaska.

SOMETHING TO THINK ABOUT: As a child, I loved to watch my mother cook. When I was 3 years old, I begged my mother to let me cook. With her help, I made an easy potato casserole. After all of the rave reviews from my family, I was hooked. I have loved cooking and have had an enthusiastic interest in cooking since that day. My mother and my mother-in-law have been great cooks, and I have gleaned much from their mentorship. I have read hundreds of cookbooks. Wherever we have lived, I have tried to learn from the best cooks in our churches. My favorite TV channel is the Food Network. It must be stated, though, that the root of my fascination for cooking has always been my love for delicious food.

Our growth in prayer follows a similar pattern to my growth in cooking: We can increase our effectiveness in prayer by observing and listening to others pray, by experiencing other kinds of prayer mentorship, by hearing sermons, by reading books, and by going to conferences—all on prayer. However, the most advantageous way to motivate improvement in our prayer lives is to have a sincere hunger and thirst after our Father God, which stems out of our great love for Him.

PRAYER EXERCISE: In your devotional time, pray the Lord's Prayer, and list the seven summarized steps. Stop after each sentence, and individualize your own personal response of prayer to add to each one. Write the seven steps in your journal. As you pray the Lord's Prayer, it will become a pattern for growth in your prayer life and not just a memorized repetition.

> *Jeremiah 21:12 (NIV) Then you will call on Me and come and pray to Me, and I will listen to you.*

Praying Specific and General Prayers

1Timothy 2:1 I urge you, first of all, to pray for all people. Ask God to help them; intercede on their behalf, and give thanks for them.

"May God open our eyes to see what the holy ministry of intercession is, to which, as His royal priesthood, we have been set apart. May He give us a large and strong heart to believe what mighty influence our prayers can exert."

–Andrew Murray

L ong before Galileo first saw the four moons of Jupiter in his telescope and Robert Hooke discovered bacteria from pond scum in his microscope, God already knew. The unending realms of the universe and the infinitesimal details of life and matter, still full of mysteries for us, are no surprise to Him. They are both His amazing handiwork.

Unlike God, Who sees the big and the little, our prayer view is usually focused only toward those people or things we can see with our eyes or hear about with our ears. We often pray only for those closest in our sphere of relationship. Though God cares very much about our "near-sighted" prayers, He wants us to have distance vision, too. Jesus challenged His disciples to move past their perspectives of self-focus when He admonished them, "Lift up your eyes, and see that the fields are white for harvest" (John 4:35b). You and I must do the same. There is a world of immense need beyond our doorstep that we must not forget.

Moving past the specific

Do you ever feel that your prayers are anemic or ineffective when praying those "far-sighted" general prayers? I read a book on prayer once that espoused that idea. I searched the Bible to see what God thought about the matter. Evidently, God didn't agree because I was surprised at the number of general prayers we are instructed to pray. Consider this list that I collected from the Scriptures:

1. Pray for all people (1Timothy 2:1).

137

2. Pray for kings and others in authority (1Timothy 2:2).

3. Pray that we may lead a quiet and peaceful life in all godliness and honesty (1Timothy 2:2).

4. Pray for those who are imprisoned, including those who are mistreated for Christ (Hebrews 13:3; Acts 12:5).

5. Pray for those who persecute you (Matthew 5:44).

6. Pray that we may escape those things coming on the Earth and be able to stand before the Son of Man (Luke 21:36).

7. Pray that God will send laborers for the harvest (Matthew 9:38).

8. Pray for the healing of our land (2 Chronicles 7:14).

9. Pray for the peace of Jerusalem (Psalm 122:6).

10. Pray for all believers (Ephesians 6:18).

11. Pray for God's Kingdom to come and His will to be done on Earth as it is in Heaven (Matthew 6:10).

If God says general prayers matter to Him, then *our* opinions don't matter. Our job is simply to pray. We can, however, pray specific things within those general categories that will empower our prayers to be more effective. On occasion, the Lord will even begin to give us strategies, not only about which to pray, but also to take action on.

God uses general categories in our prayers to make a difference. Though we cannot see the diverse tribes of Africa or the outlying farm communities of China, God sees. He hears our prayers for people on the other side of the world. It is hard for us to understand that every prayer is valuable to our Father. Even though we may feel like we are shooting aimlessly in the dark, we are hitting the mark of Heaven.

True Story: Such has been the case of a prayer ministry focus the Lord has given to me called "Prodigal Monday." Bruce and I began meeting so many hurting parents in our travels who asked us to pray for their children. As a result, the Lord burdened my heart to set aside a specific day of prayer in behalf of this need. Each Monday, I send a general prayer request for prodigals and their families with accompanying scriptures for partners to use in prayer. It is sent by text or email to friends and is also posted on several Facebook group pages. Since its launch, the Lord has brought many prodigals, parents of prodigals, and former prodigals into my path. Two weeks after the prayer emphasis began, a family member that had been a prodigal for 35 years came back to the Lord. It was a confirmation to me that it is a matter that touches our Father's heart and should be a subject of our regular intercession.

True Story: In the early 1990s, a call went out to intercessors to begin praying for the 10/40 window. This area of the world extends from 10 degrees north to 40 degrees north of the equator and from West Africa to East Asia. It is an area that has seen more suffering than any other since the time of Christ and, at that time, had been least touched by the Gospel. It was a prayer initiative that was aimed to continue until the year 2000. Many prayer organizations and denominations began to link together in prayer for this region of the world. Their endeavor was called "Praying Through the Window."

Since that organized prayer effort, there has been an amazing increase of missionaries who have accepted the call to go to the nations within that region. There has also been a supernatural increase of people coming to faith in Christ from this area of the world. At the time of this writing, the top ten countries where Christianity is growing the fastest are in the 10/40 window. This is the powerful result of God's people praying in unity.[12]

SOMETHING TO THINK ABOUT: Sometimes God takes the general prayers we are praying and begins to bring people into our lives that our prayers are impacting. This helps us to see how our prayers are making a difference and enables us to further understand details about which we should be praying. For instance, many times I have prayed in a general way for missionaries. As the Lord has brought specific missionaries into my life, my knowledge of their sacrifices and their challenges has increased. It has reminded me that my prayers have real faces, real needs, and real importance.

PRAYER EXERCISE: Write these eleven general prayer categories in your prayer journal. Pray through this list today. As you do, the Lord may give you some specifics to pray about within each group. For instance, when praying for all people everywhere (1 Timothy 2:1), I try to pray for the salvation of unbelievers. I pray for people who are institutionalized in nursing homes, hospitals, orphanages, prisons, mental institutions, and drug rehabilitation centers. I also pray for the poor, the grieving, the homeless, the hurting, the abused, and the enslaved. As I pray for those in authority over us, I try to remember our government leaders, our law enforcement officers, our firefighters, our military, our homeland security, and our secret service agencies. When praying for all believers, I pray for the church at large, for church leaders, including apostles, prophets, evangelists, pastors, missionaries, and teachers. I also include laborers who serve alongside those leaders and Christians who are suffering for the cause of Christ. General prayers matter to God and are increased in effectiveness as we add specifics to them.

Psalm 22:24 For he has not despised or abhorred the affliction of the afflicted, and he has not hidden his face from him, but has heard, when he cried to him.

2 Chronicles 7:14(NIV) If my people, who are called by my name, will humble themselves and pray and seek my face and turn from their wicked ways, then I will hear from heaven, and I will forgive their sin and will heal their land.

Praying for Myself

Psalm 61:2 Hear my cry, O God, listen to my prayer; from the end of the earth I call to you when my heart is faint. Lead me to the rock that is higher than I.

"Time spent alone with God is not wasted. It changes us; it changes our surroundings; and every Christian who would live the life that counts, and who would have power for service must take time to pray."

-M.E. Andross

Many psychologists believe that a person who has no self-love is incapable of loving others. Jesus, the author of life and the personification of love, established this important principle when He said, *"Love thy neighbor as thyself."* An excellent parallel in line with Jesus' command for loving others as we love ourselves, added to the Apostle Paul's directive to pray for all people, is to **pray** for our neighbor **as** we pray for **ourselves**.

Most of us feel that we are being too self-focused when we pray for ourselves. I remember on one anniversary getaway, Bruce and I were visiting Bellingrath Gardens near Mobile, Alabama. We noticed that a worker tending to a flowerbed nearby was having a physical struggle. When we greeted this lady, she apologized for all of her groaning and moaning; she had not realized we were nearby. When we asked if we might pray for her, she thanked us but declined our offer saying that God had much bigger things He needed to take care of than her arthritis. We insisted and took a few minutes to pray for Jan. Most of us, like Jan, make the mistake of thinking we might bother God with our own personal needs since we have submitted so many requests for others.

Prayer for oneself serves an important purpose. When done correctly, prayer brings transformation, not only in the ones being prayed for but in the one who is praying. The more we pray, the more like Jesus we should become. In order to be more like Jesus, we must pray for the "me" that others see as well as the "me" only God can see.

David prayed for himself many times in the book of Psalms. He prayed for the secret areas of his heart and life to be exposed to God (Psalm 19:13,14; 139:23,24). He prayed for God's help in making important spiritual changes necessary (Psalm 51; 120:2; 141:3).

David prayed for his steps to be ordered by God (Psalm 119:133). He prayed about his emotional highs and his lows (Psalm 138:3; Psalm 61:1,2). He prayed about the enemies he was facing (Psalm 18:47,48: Psalm 102:8; Psalm 3). He prayed that God's Word would have a greater reign in his life (Psalm 19; Psalm 119).

If we are going to be significant influencers in the world around us, we, like David, must be bold enough to say, "God show me the things you see that I need to address and change in my life." We should also pray for God to develop and strengthen our abilities so we can do greater things for His glory. To remain holy in a culture of ever-changing morals, we must regularly pray that we can recognize good from evil, right from wrong.

Jesus instructed his disciples to pray several things concerning themselves. *"Watch and pray that you may not enter into temptation"* (Matthew 26:41a). *"Pray always that you may be counted worthy to escape all these things that will come to pass and to stand before the Son of Man"* (Luke 21:36, NKJV). Speaking of His return, He warned, *"Watch and pray for you do not know when the time is"* (Mark 13:33, NKJV).

Praying for oneself results in healing for our bodies (Jeremiah 17:14; Psalm 30:2) and restoration of our emotional wounds (Psalm 41:4). It makes dreaming God-sized dreams and accomplishing God-sized achievements possible (Psalm18:29-34). Prayers for oneself can increase the circumference of our influence, renew our effectiveness, and provide blessings and opportunities that are God-given and God-driven.

True Stories: God anointed my dad, Paul Radke, and my father-in-law, Lamar Headley, to represent Him in many powerful arenas, though each was unique and different. Both have been men of prayer and faith. Each started from humble beginnings but God raised them up to be influential for His Kingdom. Our dads have prayed for divine opportunities and open doors so they could be used strategically for eternal purposes. Their wives, our mothers, have also been great women of prayer and service, and have significantly helped to increase our dads' effectiveness.

My dad was a pastor who cared deeply about unbelievers and ministered to people of high and low degree in his community. He reached thousands through radio and television. God also gave him the privilege of being salt and light in the political arena. Because he was faithful to pray at every humble occasion offered to him, God blessed him with great opportunities on influential platforms. He prayed at two gubernatorial inaugurations and prayed the opening prayer for a session of the United States House of Representatives. He was passionate to share the message of salvation within each one of those prayers, whether it was praying a blessing over a newly planted tree on Arbor Day or beseeching God for His wisdom at an important inaugural celebration.

My father-in-law, Lamar, served in a national leadership position, helping to inspire and empower young people to become missionaries, using his influence to get them to their field of service. He enlisted the help of hundreds of retirees, volunteers, and construction teams to use their important skills for the work of God in building Bible schools and churches here in the United States and around the world. Lamar has also served on national and international boards that were instrumental in many people coming to Christ through healthcare ministry and drug-recovery programs. Most recently, he and my mother-in-law, Jimmie Ruth, pastored international churches (in Japan and Cambodia) on short-term missionary assignments. Only eternity will reveal the exponential returns from the impact of their lives for the Kingdom of Heaven.

True Story: My mother had many testimonies of God healing her body as a result of others' prayers, as well as her own. At one point, she was scheduled at the hospital to have a lumpectomy. The doctor had already done a biopsy and knew the lump in her breast was cancerous. The day before her surgery, while at home washing her hair, she began boldly singing, "I am healed by the stripes that He bore," a song she had learned as a child. Working the shampoo through her hair, she continued to sing with all of her heart. Reaching out by faith to God in that moment, she felt a strong surge of the power of God flow through her. She knew God had healed her, and she began to praise the Lord excitedly as shampoo went all over the room. The lump was completely gone!

The doctor's office called the next day when she did not show up to the hospital as scheduled. As my mother explained to the nurse how the Lord had healed her, the doctor personally got on the phone. He insisted my mother was to come right in and get checked, stating, "this is a very serious matter." She agreed and went in at his request. The amazed doctor confirmed that the lump was completely gone, never to return.

SOMETHING TO THINK ABOUT: The prayer of Jabez is evidence of how one man's prayers for himself brought a divine turnaround. Jabez's name actually means "pain," which infers that he caused his mother pain in childbirth. He didn't let that label stop him, though.

Remember that regardless of how others have regarded you, their opinions hold no authority with God. Scripture shows that He has good plans and a good future stored up for you (Jeremiah 29:11). Like Jabez, we must simply be bold enough to ask God for His blessings and His favor.

> *1 Chronicles 4:10 (NKJV) And Jabez called upon the God of Israel, saying, "Oh, that you would bless me indeed, and enlarge my territory, that Your hand would be with me, and that You would keep me from evil, that I may not cause pain!" So God granted him what he requested.*

PRAYER EXERCISE: Today, pray through Psalm 19:12-14; Psalm 139:23,24; Psalm 119:133 (written below) and 1 Chronicles 4:10 (written above). Pray them with sincerity and personalize them as you read them. Ask God to accomplish greater things in you for His glory. Use these and other scriptures to remind yourself and the Lord of the things you desire for Him to do in your life. Write them in your journal so you will have quick access to them in your times of prayer.

Psalm 19:12-14(NLV) "Who can see his own mistakes? Forgive my sins that I do not see. And keep Your servant from sinning by going my own way. Do not let these sins rule over me. Then I will be without blame. And I will not be found guilty of big sins. Let the words of my mouth and the thoughts of my heart be pleasing in Your eyes, O Lord, my Rock and the One Who saves me."

Psalm 139:23,24 Search me, O God, and know my heart! Try me and know my thoughts! And see if there be any grievous way in me, and lead me in the way everlasting!

Psalm 119:133 Guide my steps by your word, so I will not be overcome by evil.

Praying with My Spouse

Colossians 1:17 And he is before all things, and in him all things hold together.

"For over 30 years of marriage we have ended each day in prayer together as a couple. No spiritual discipline has protected our marriage and our family more than this daily time of communion together with God."

–Dennis and Barbara Rainey

God established a precedence of relationship by His one-on-one companionship with Adam in the Garden of Eden. When Eve was created, she, too, was given the privilege of fellowship with God. Daily communion with their Creator brought guidance and purpose to their lives as individuals and as a couple. Today, our Heavenly Father's desire remains the same for us: a one-on-one relationship with Him and a vital place of daily fellowship and direction within our marriage, also.

Adam and Eve's companionship with God was ruined by their sin in the Garden of Eden. The residual effects of their disobedience brought misery and dissension into their marriage. The curse fell hard upon Adam to work by the sweat of his brow. Besides the pain of childbirth, Eve would also struggle with the "you will desire to control your husband, but he will rule over you" part of the curse (Genesis 3:16b), causing the constant tug-of-war that often plagues our marriages.

Dissension in marriage perhaps began with the "blame game." Adam blamed Eve for giving him the fruit, though Eve knew firsthand that Adam was standing right there with her; he didn't prevent or contest her handing him the fruit (Genesis 3:6). If they verbalized so freely in front of God, one wonders what they did in private. Someone jokingly pictured Adam walking in front of the Garden of Eden, which was guarded by two angels and a flaming sword. His children inquired, "What is that place, Daddy?" Adam replied, "Kids, that is where your mother ate us out of house and home!"

Marriage was created by God to be a picture of unity. "The two shall become one," the Scripture says. When you and I include God in the equation of our marriage, our oneness is increased. As we put God first, we see the return of the beautiful plan that He initially intended for us.

Some might think making God a priority in our marriage would be "three's a crowd" thinking. Statistics have shown, however, that praying together as a couple greatly diminishes the divorce factor. Surprisingly, it also increases the emotional and physical satisfaction of both partners in the marriage. [13]

How to make it work

How to pray together will be a decision you and your spouse must make jointly. You may begin this new adventure by praying silently with each other or by saying a few sentences aloud together each day, increasing as you become more comfortable. Holding hands or some other form of contact while praying is unifying and bonding. The important thing is to at least start somewhere if both of you are willing.

My husband Bruce and I usually have our individual devotions in the morning and pray together in the evening. We begin by reading aloud or listening to the Bible (on smart phone app) together. This allows the Word of God to renew our minds. Afterward, we each share specific requests about which we would like the other to pray. We also have a list of things we pray over daily. Usually, we take turns praying aloud for each other, our family, our friends, our prayer partners, our extended relationships, matters of our nation, and finally, our world.

For those who are new to praying together (and perhaps feeling overwhelmed at this point), it is important to remember:

- To do your best to express your desires for praying together without pressure.
- Not to feel discouraged if it takes your spouse some time to warm up to the idea.

- Any efforts, even small beginnings, will be beneficial to your marriage and pleasing to God.

Many people initially feel very inadequate and intimidated at the thought of praying aloud. Try taking small steps such as praying the Lord's Prayer together. Do your best to be consistent, and you will see a wonderful habit develop.

Praying *for* each other is also important and is valuable, whether you are side by side or a hundred miles away from your spouse. Here are some topics of prayer to consider when praying alone or together for your husband or wife: their journey with God, their health, their relationships, their challenges, their roles and responsibilities, their divine destiny and purpose. Even if your spouse is not yet open to praying together, you can personally pray for them and your marriage, and God will hear.

True Story: During a weekend visit, my friend and prayer partner, Denise, tearfully opened up to me that her husband, Chad, had a problem with alcohol. She confided that even though he was a faithful church attender, it was an issue that had persisted in their marriage for many years. I was the first person she had ever told.

Denise's husband seemed totally unaware his drinking was even a problem. Though violence had never been an issue, alcohol affected Chad's personality in a very negative way. It was something that had distressed my friend for most of their marriage.

Denise and I began that night to pray together about the matter. We prayed Psalm 139:5 that God would hem Chad in, behind and before, and lay His hand upon Chad, taking the desire for alcohol out of him.

The next day, Chad called Denise to tell her that he had been in a car accident. Though Chad's shoulder was injured, he insisted Denise stay with me and enjoy her visit since he was recovering safely at home, and her visit was nearing the end.

Denise and I committed to continuing to pray about Chad's drinking. When she returned home, Denise learned that the pain medication her husband had been prescribed could not be mixed with alcohol. (God was hemming him in.) During the time of Chad's recovery, Denise shared her heart with her husband. She revealed her true feelings about his drinking and the changes she saw in him when he used alcohol. Denise asked Chad not to drink anymore. She also requested for the two of them to have devotions together each morning. Chad hesitantly agreed to both.

Chad and Denise began to pray faithfully and read the Word together. They prayed about the real issues pressing in on their marriage. They prayed about Chad's health and their family. Recently, Chad and Denise celebrated the second anniversary of Chad's freedom from alcohol. As a result of his abstinence, Chad's health greatly improved: he was able to get off all of his blood pressure medications. He lost 40 pounds; his cholesterol went back to normal, and his mobility and endurance increased. God has done amazing things in Denise and Chad's marriage, in their spiritual walk together, and in Chad's health as a result of prayer.

SOMETHING TO THINK ABOUT: Everything God created in the beginning, was good except for one thing: God saw it was *"not good that man should be alone"* (Genesis 2:18, NKJV). Marriage was God's perfect solution for that which was imperfect. Interestingly, our Heavenly Father did not choose to fill man's loneliness with another male friend so they could go hunting and fishing together. Rather, God created a female counterpart who would complete him. Eve was a gift to Adam, and Adam was a gift to Eve. This amazing partnership God invented also has some wonderful possibilities for us in the realm of prayer.

1. The intimacy of marriage provides a safe environment for the fulfillment of James 5:16, *"Therefore, confess your faults to one another and pray that you may be healed."*

2. Marriage also provides the unity needed for the fulfillment of Matthew 18:19, *"If two of you agree on earth about anything they ask, it will be done for them by my Father in heaven."*

God provided within our marriage a ready-made prayer partner, to have and to hold, who cares about our needs on a level that few others can understand.

PRAYER EXERCISE:

If you and your spouse do not presently pray together, ask the Lord to show you the right time to introduce the idea to your spouse. Consider researching the topic of praying together in marriage so you will have a greater knowledge on the subject when the right time arrives.

Whether or not you and your spouse already pray together, commit to pray for your spouse in a greater way every day. Make a list in your journal as God brings to your mind the things you should be praying. Consider including those things discussed in this chapter. Add scripture promises within your list, and thank God for His provision of every need. Your prayers for your spouse touch the heart of God and provide an entry point for your prayers together.

Genesis 25:2 (NIV) Isaac prayed to the Lord on behalf of his wife, because she was childless. The Lord answered his prayer, and his wife Rebekah became pregnant.

Praying with My Children

Matthew 19:14 Let the little children come to me, and do not hinder them, for the kingdom of heaven belongs to such as these.

"Age doesn't matter. God is passionate about encountering children, and for so long children have been held back from the deep things of God...God longs to bring children into the fullness of who He is. That is where they've always belonged. All over the earth, God is revealing Himself to the young."

– Jennifer Toledo

From a very early age, children have the ability to know and encounter God. My mother, Ruth Pruitt Radke, shared her story with me of how she came to salvation at the age of 5. She vividly remembered the day she was playing in the yard outside her home when she felt the great burden of her sin. In her guilt of her wrongdoing, she began to repeat, "Oh God, Oh God, Oh God," but didn't really know how to pray. When she walked into the kitchen, her mother overheard her words and saw the troubled look on her face. The Spirit of the Lord prompted my grandmother and she said, "Ruthie, have you ever prayed and asked Jesus to be your Savior?" My mother responded that she did not know how. My grandmother prayed with her right then and led her in a prayer of repentance and commitment to Jesus. Then my sweet little mother went skipping out of the house. In retrospect, she still recalled how "It felt like the weight of the world had lifted off my shoulders."

Bruce and I began leading our children in prayer individually as soon as they could repeat words. Both of our children asked to receive the Lord into their hearts at young ages. Early in their lives they amazed us with their strong spiritual perceptions and understandings. Near the end of age 2 our daughter Bethany said, "Mommy, (I) want Jesus in here" (as she pointed to her heart). Joyfully, I led her in a simple prayer for salvation. When my son Stephen was near the same age, he came over to pray for me as I sat on the floor. I was feeling somewhat feverish and dizzy. "Dear Jees," (Jesus), he prayed, "touch Mommy. Top head, soz (soles) feet. Buke (Rebuke) Devil! Jees name. Amen!"

God healed us and spoke so many times through the prayers and words of our children. The same has been true of our granddaughter, Tuesday, who received Jesus early into her life and has had so many amazing spiritual insights she has shared with us. Children have a great capacity to believe God and have faith in Him. That is why Jesus said as we approach God, we must come as a little child. We know God speaks to children and their prayers are powerful in touching Heaven.

It is important to teach our children God's Word, to initiate times of prayer with them, and then to follow up by doing all that we can to nurture and encourage their personal relationship to God. It is also vital that we live out the things we teach. Children are like spiritual sponges. They will absorb whatever is around them. We must provide the spiritual tools and teachings that will help them grow to be strong Christians, all in an atmosphere of love and kindness.

True Story: One Saturday evening when our children were small, I was working on my music for our church service the following day. Since Bruce was working on his sermon in the other room, both children were with me. As I practiced the song, "In the Presence of Jehovah," on the piano, the presence of God overwhelmingly filled our small living room. Stephen, about 8 months old, was in a little sit-up seat near me. He began to give an unusual soft cry or vocalization that I had never heard before. I finished my song and in a hushed voice, I asked our 3-year-old who was near him, "Why is Stephen crying, Bethany?" She responded, "Mommy, I think he feels the presence of the Lord." It was exactly what I had felt in my heart. I was amazed at Bethany's spiritual perception of the situation. Both a baby and a small child were able to discern the presence of the Lord who visited us on that special evening.

True Story: When our children were little, we would usually have a boys' night/girls' night each week. Bethany and I would spend the night in the kids' room and Stephen and Bruce would spend the night in our bedroom. We would always tell stories of special interest to each child on those evenings.

One such time I had been suffering from a severe headache. Nothing was helping. I had persevered through our special activities since it was our special family night. When we went to bed, I tried, but couldn't be my usual self because I felt so terrible. Bethany was very sweet to understand that I could not entertain her with our usual story time. All was quiet in the house. It appeared the boys' conversations in the other room had ended, also.

Bethany was asleep as I lay there in the dark wondering how I was going to get to sleep with my head throbbing so fiercely. As I cried out to God, I heard the pitter patter of little footsteps from the other room. Stephen, just barely 3, came over to me in the dark. He put his little hand on me and prayed, "Jesus, please heal Mommy. Take her headache away." As quickly as he came, he left, and miraculously my headache left, also. It was as if it drained right out of me from my head to my toes. It was such a miracle that I could hardly believe it! In an instant, I went from intense pain to being completely pain-free. That night, I slept like a baby because of my child's prayer.

SOMETHING TO THINK ABOUT: Teaching children about God should not be a miserable, stiff, and starchy event. In our home, our children did puzzles, played with toys, or did artwork as Bruce read to us from the Bible. We also played Bible games or did puppets as other methods of teaching Bible stories. When we prayed, we did so individually and collectively as a family.

The Bible shows that we are to teach our children the commandments of God in the process of life. *"You shall teach them diligently to your children and shall talk of them when you sit in your house, and when you walk by the way, and when you lie down and when you rise" (Deuteronomy 6:7).* Prayer and biblical instruction are intended by God to be a natural part of the flow of our family interaction. God has built strong spiritual receptors into our children. We, as parents, must guide their understanding and development as God works in them.

PRAYER EXERCISE: If praying with your children is a new step, sharing a brief story of the personal impact of prayer in your own life may be a good place to start. Initially, you may want to lead by example as your children listen to your prayers for them. After a few weeks or when they are old enough, assist them as they repeat a simple prayer after you, a few words, a phrase, or a sentence at a time. Encourage them to construct their own prayers (with some assistance from you, if needed) as they become more knowledgeable and confident. In time, give your children a prayer journal and teach them how to use it. Have them write their prayer needs, special scriptures, and the answers to prayers they have received, along with their thanks and praises to God.

> *2 Timothy 1:5 (NIV) I have been reminded of your sincere faith, which first lived in your grandmother...and in your mother...and, I am persuaded, now lives in you, also.*

> *Matthew 21:16 (NLT) They asked Jesus, "Do you hear what these children are saying?" "Yes," Jesus replied. "Haven't you ever read the Scriptures? For they say, 'You have taught children and infants to give you praise.'"*

Praying for My Children

1 Samuel 1:27,28 (NIV) I prayed for this child, and the Lord has granted me what I asked of him. So now I give him to the Lord. For his whole life he will be given over to the Lord.

"Pray consistently for your family...let them know you are praying for them...and you care deeply about what happens to them. Most of all pray that they will open their hearts and lives to Jesus Christ and become His followers."

–Billy Graham, Nearing Home.

"As you pray for your children each day, your prayer of faith will go before them and open the right doors—the God-planned doors—and close the ones that would be detrimental to God's purpose for their lives."

–George Sawyer, The Daniel Prayer for Parents

Our children will never come to the place where they do not need our prayers. Even before they are born, they need us to be praying for them. I know the truth of that statement, personally, because Bruce and I still greatly need his parents' prayers. My parents are now in Heaven, but I still petition the Lord to answer the prayers they prayed for us, which I believe have remained as a memorial before Him (Acts 10:4; 1 Kings 8:59).

As a parent I always believed when my children left our home, my prayer responsibilities would lighten in respect to my intercession for them. Little did I realize, the importance of prayer only escalates when our children become independent. Whereas we previously had a voice in our children's lives in decision-making and guidance, we now have powerful influence with God on their behalf. Through prayer, God will bring His intervention, protection, wisdom, and guidance in their lives.

Thankfully, God loves our children even more than we do. The stories of Abraham, Rebekah, Hagar, and Hannah are just a few that give evidence God hears our questions and our prayers concerning our children. The scriptural concept of the fatherhood of God and His love for us, His children, also comforts us that He understands our deepest concerns for them.

We, as parents, are responsible for teaching and training our children in the ways of righteousness while they are in our homes. It is our place to set an example before them as we follow the Lord. Ultimately, however, there are certain things that only God can do for our children.

Though Hannah could keep her vow to God to "loan" her son, Samuel, to the Lord, only God could personally solidify the relationship with Samuel by speaking to him. Consider Jochabed. She could do her best to try to save Moses' life by making the little buoyant basket, but only God could finish the job by providing the Egyptian princess to raise him. Later, on the backside of the desert, God, alone, could provide the burning bush that led Moses to his destiny.

Through prayer, we as parents share a partnership with our Heavenly Father. One day while watching a Christian television program, I saw a minister being interviewed who had been delivered from many years of addiction. This man shared how faithfully his mother prayed for him through the years of his prodigal ways. One day in exasperation he shouted out to God, "Leave me alone!" At that moment, he clearly heard the voice of the Lord respond, "When your mother leaves me alone, I will leave you alone!"

Jesus is the Author and Finisher of our faith and of our children's faith also. As New Testament believers, we are heirs of the promises of God found in the Old Testament. In those Books, God says that He will teach our children (Isaiah 54:12-14), that He will give them a heart to worship Him (Jeremiah 32:39), and that He will discipline them (Psalm 89:30-34). These are just a few of the things we must earnestly and faithfully seek the Lord to do in our children's lives.

As mentioned before, these scriptures do not mean we as parents can shirk our responsibility to follow God's command to train our children when they are in our homes. When we have done our best, though, we have to diligently pray and trust God that He will do the rest.

True Story: Bruce's Granddaddy Horton was a great prayer intercessor. He would rise early each Sunday morning to pray for his family in ministry: his grandsons, Bruce and Gregg, his son, Morris, and his son-in-law, Lamar, who were all pastors or in ministry leadership positions. Granddaddy had been a pastor, himself, and he knew how much he depended on prayer. For many Sundays after his Granddaddy Horton's death, Bruce thought of how much he missed knowing his grandfather's prayers were being lifted heavenward for him.

When the Lord turned our road from the pastorate into a traveling ministry, Bruce began to feel compelled to support other pastors by praying for them, extending the prayer covering that he has received these years from our parents and grandparents. He has told me, "I don't want any of our pastors going to the pulpit wondering if anyone has prayed for them."

True Story: In the second half of our son Stephen's senior year of high school, a series of unusual and mysterious, unrelated health issues began to occur on and off for the duration of one year:

The first was a noticeable drooping of his eye which turned out to be a nerve condition called Horner's syndrome. Though God healed him, Stephen's senior pictures still give noticeable evidence of that journey. Following his graduation, while at a summer camp, Stephen was rushed to the emergency room, and then hospitalized with pericarditis, an infection of the lining of his heart. Though he recovered within a week from that sickness, he was diagnosed with mononucleosis, shortly thereafter. Miraculously, through answered prayer, he went back to camp as a counselor two weeks later.

In the Fall, Stephen enrolled for his freshman year at a college in Texas. He remained in great health until January when, after attending a wedding, he became very ill with vomiting and stomach pain. At one point, violent chills with uncontrollable shaking took over his entire body. He had experienced these same symptoms with pericarditis in the hospital when his potassium level dropped very low. (Amazingly, several years prior to both of these incidents, the Lord had directed my reading to an article stating that orange juice is one of the quickest food substances to ingest in treating a potassium deficiency.) Within minutes after drinking the hotel orange juice, Stephen ceased shaking. However, the issue with his stomach pain continued to escalate. In the early morning hours, he begged us to take him to the emergency room.

That night, Dallas was completely shut down because of an ice storm. Praying constantly, we drove as fast as we could in those terrible conditions to get to the hospital. Stephen was crying out to God and screaming in pain all the way—totally unlike our son, who had never been overly dramatic even when he was suffering.

Immediately upon pulling up to the emergency room, Stephen jumped out of the car, ran into the building, and fell on the floor of the entryway writhing in pain. The staff rushed to him as he screamed, begging for their help. I followed anxiously as they made their way down the hall to examine him. Bruce hurried to park the car.

The medical staff instantly went to work. Initially, they thought Stephen was having a drug overdose. Once they were confident he was not, the staff asked careful questions relating to other gastronomical issues. Meanwhile, I could sense changes happening in Stephen as they questioned him. Visibly, the strain of intense suffering had vanished from his face. When they asked him about his pain level, he said it had been a ten but had just dropped to zero. No pain was a good sign, but it was also a bad sign since a burst appendix can sometimes bring an immediate sensation of relief.

Blood tests and extensive imaging were ordered. Stephen was released hours later after they were assured he was stable and the mysterious crisis was past. From that point on, he had no pain and experienced no further symptoms. God had once again done a miracle for our son.

SOMETHING TO THINK ABOUT: *Isaiah 43:26 says, "Put me in remembrance; let us argue together; set forth your case, that you may be proved right."* This is essentially what Abraham did in behalf of his nephew, Lot, and his

160

family in Genesis 18. You and I have the same privilege to pray, seek, and remind the Lord of His covenant with us, and plead with Him in behalf of our children and our grandchildren.

PRAYER EXERCISE: As we pray for our loved ones, it is important to ask God for specific things just as Abraham did. Remember, he asked God to save Lot and his family from the destruction about to be rained upon Sodom. Pray today for your children and grandchildren, also. Write their names in your journal. Search the Bible for passages and promises to place alongside them. You can bring these things to the Lord's remembrance as you pray for your family.

It is important for us, as parents, also to rest our hearts upon scriptures of encouragement. Place these passages in a prominent place in your journal. We must build ourselves up with these promises of God as we trust and lean upon Him at all times.

> *Psalm 102:28 The children of your servants shall dwell secure; and their offspring shall be established before you.*
>
> *Jeremiah 32:39 And I will give them one heart and one purpose to worship me forever, for their own good and for the good of all their descendants.*
>
> *Psalm 90:16 Let your work be shown to your servants and your glorious power to their children.*
>
> *Isaiah 54:11 All your children shall be taught by the Lord, and great shall be the peace of your children.*

SECTION 7

WHAT CAN I DO WHILE I AM WAITING?

When God Puts You on Hold

Psalm 27:14 Wait for the Lord; be strong, and let your heart take courage; wait for the Lord!

"Delayed answers to prayer are not only trials of faith, but they give us opportunities of honoring God by our steadfast confidences in Him under apparent repulses."

-C.H. Spurgeon

It seems like every time I call the airlines, the pharmacy, or the bookstore, I am put on hold. It is always a temptation just to hang up, but I know I will lose my turn and then have to start all over again.

It is easy to feel this way when we pray—that we are somehow in a Heavenly lineup waiting our turn for our prayers to be answered. We are tempted to just give up, but we know quitting is not the answer.

Jairus, a temple ruler in Jesus' day, must have known this feeling when he asked Jesus to hurry and come pray for his little daughter who lay dying. He and Jesus were making good progress toward his house when a woman in the crowd, sick for twelve years, reached out in faith and got her miracle (Luke 8:43).

It was in that moment that Jesus put Jairus on hold or "take a number," so to speak, in order to assess the situation. I am sure Jairus rejoiced for this woman who had been sick for so long, but he must have been thinking, "Hurry Jesus! Don't you remember my little daughter is dying?"

It is hard to understand God's delays in answering our own prayer concerns. "Could you work faster, Lord? Could you focus your attention on me for just a moment to address my emergency?" It takes a lot of trust and patience to remain in a holding pattern.

It would have been easy for Jairus to perceive Jesus as insensitive or uncaring, especially when his servant brought the news to him that it was too late; his daughter had already died. It must have felt like an eternity before they finally arrived at Jairus' home.

We, too, sometimes experience those same desperate feelings when the answer doesn't come as quickly as we thought. Why is it that God's schedule and our timelines are seldom matching? There is often a period of praying, of waiting, and of trusting. It is hard to understand at times why God's ways and timing are best.

Jairus could have gone home after hearing the bad news of his daughter's death, but he didn't. It is easy to get discouraged, give up, and leave the Miracle Worker before our miracle has manifested. The Bible shows us that the secret is in quieting our hearts and holding steady. Psalm 46:10 instructs us, "Be still and know that I am God."

You see, there are many people now, and there were many people then, who got disillusioned with Jesus and quit following Him. They didn't like it because He didn't do things their way. One day after a large group defected, Jesus asked the twelve disciples, "Do you want to go away as well?" Peter's response is one that you and I should hold to steadfastly in times of disillusionment or delay: *"Lord, to whom shall we go? You have the words of eternal life"* (John 6:68).

Like Peter, Jairus knew Jesus was the only one with the answers. He had faith that Jesus would ultimately turn things around and He did. In the end, it turned out for a bigger miracle and a better finale. Jairus' daughter was raised from the dead, and the entire region heard the story. You and I are inspired by it today.

While we wait, God is doing something *in us*. Our faith deepens. Our trust grows. Our endurance turns to perseverance. In the end, God plans a bigger finish and He accomplishes more.

"When God delays, He is not inactive. He is getting ready His instruments, He is ripening our powers; and at the appointed moment we shall arise equal to our task. Even Jesus of Nazareth was thirty years in privacy, growing in wisdom before He began His work." – Dr. Jowett[14]

Proverbs 3:5 Trust in the Lord with all your heart, and do not lean on your own understanding.

True Story: My friend, Kitty, grew up in a Christian home. As she entered high school and college, however, she lost her faith. Kitty became driven by feminist philosophies of the late sixties and her atheistic beliefs biased her thinking in all areas of life. Ethel, Kitty's mom, could not understand her youngest daughter's new perspectives and especially her spiritual desertion of the God she had known and loved as a child. Ethel prayed faithfully for her precious daughter, year after year.

As Kitty grew older, she and her mom drew closer to each other with each passing day, but Ethel's prayers and words seemed to be to no avail. The divine turn finally happened in the year 2000. In the wake of her 87-year-old mother's death, Kitty longed to know if there was a possibility of ever seeing her mother again. Her heart was later stirred as she read something in her mother's journal: "I look forward to death, except for one reason only. How can I possibly live in a world, no matter how heavenly it may be, if my little agnostic Kitty is not there?" Kitty began a desperate quest to see if her mother's "imaginary friend" and the Heaven she looked forward to might be real.

As a *summa cum laude* journalism graduate and a freelance science writer, Kitty was well familiar with the viewpoint and biases of secular science. She was not familiar, however, with the amazing scientific evidence and research that points clearly to a divine Creator. This time, she contemplated both sides of the argument. She also studied the world's major religions and finally the Bible. Guided by the God of her childhood and empowered by her mother's prayers, Kitty began to see the truth emerge.

Kitty tells the story of her quest in her beautiful memoir, *Heaven Without Her* (Thomas Nelson, 2008). Today, Kitty ministers to many elderly clients in nursing homes. She also encourages many parents whose children have lost their faith.

Kitty gladly shares her amazing testimony of the journey back to her Heavenly Father who has welcomed her with His loving arms.

Kitty's life story is a reminder that God takes even the things that seem to make no sense in our lives, even His delays to our prayers, and uses them for a bigger purpose than we ever thought or imagined. But for Kitty's dear mom who has gone on ahead, the story is not over. At long last, Ethel's prayers have been answered, and she and her beloved daughter will be reunited one happy day, for all eternity.

True Story: A number of years ago, a church member in our congregation shared a recording of a powerful testimony. It was of a pastor in Texas whose voice had been silenced for two years by a virus, which affected the nerves of his vocal cords. On this recording, this man was teaching a Sunday school class, reading in a whisper from the 103rd Psalm, "Who forgives all your sins and heals all your diseases, who redeems your life from the pit." As he expounded on that verse, this pastor's voice was fully restored! My heart was so encouraged by listening to the replay of the miracle moment.

One night, years later, we were having supper with our good friend, Norm, in Springfield, Missouri. He began to share the amazing miracle of how God healed his son-in-law, Duane Miller, a number of years earlier of an incurable vocal disorder. He told of his son-in-law's challenging and discouraging journey and of the many prayers he, his family, and friends had prayed. Norm went on to give God praise that since Duane's healing, he had been given great opportunities to share his miraculous story on national television, on radio talk shows, and had spoken around the world. As I listened, I became excited as I realized this was the man's testimony I had heard years before! (Check out Nuvoice.org to hear it!)

SOMETHING TO THINK ABOUT: It is easy to lose perspective or get discouraged in our waiting. Joseph in the Old Testament is a great example that God's plan is worth the wait. Though it seemed like God had forgotten him, he still walked in excellence and obedience in the pit, at Potiphar's, in prison and at the

168

palace. Whatever the stage of your waiting or whatever you are waiting for, don't lose your patience or your hope. Help is on the way!

PRAYER EXERCISE: As you pray today, let the Lord know you trust Him, though you may not have yet received the answer to your prayer. Recount the faithfulness of God. Pray through Psalm 103:1-5. It is a reminder of the many areas in which God has blessed you in the past. Personalize it with your own stories, verse by verse. Tell the Lord you remember His faithfulness, even in the midst of your wait.

Psalm 103:1-5 Bless the Lord, O my soul, and all that is within me, bless his holy name! Bless the Lord, O my soul and forget not all his benefits, who forgives all your iniquity, who heals all your diseases, Who redeems your life from the pit, who crowns you with steadfast love and mercy, Who satisfies you with good so that your youth is renewed like the eagle's.

Galatians 6:9 And let us not grow weary in doing good, for in due season we will reap, if we do not give up.

Do the Possible

Ecclesiastes 9:10 (AMP) Whatever your hand finds to do, do it with all your might.

"Pray as though everything depended on God. Work as though everything depended on you."

-Saint Augustine

What do you do when you don't know what to do? I often tell people, "You do the possible, and trust God to do the impossible." Let me explain this further. Recently I was recovering from a cold. Besides feeling poorly, my greatest frustration was that my sense of taste was gone. I sent out a request to my family and a few friends to pray for me. Immediately afterward, I had a thought to go and try some apple cider vinegar. I wondered if this thought was from the Lord, or if it was an action that would show a lack of faith.

"You do the possible, and trust God to do the impossible," came to my mind. I followed through with a few doses within the next two hours. By lunchtime, I was feeling better and my sense of taste was completely back in order. I don't know if this was a natural remedy God gave to me or if He simply blessed my obedience.

Don't get me wrong; we mustn't get sidetracked like Abraham and Sarah, thinking the burden of accomplishment is on our shoulders. However, the Bible shows people of faith are also people of action. Consider the servants who filled the water pots at Jesus' command. They did the possible, and Jesus did the impossible by turning water into wine. Consider the sons of the widow who gathered the pots at Elisha's direction. Each and every jar ended up being filled with oil that could be sold to pay their debts. They did the possible. God did the impossible. Consider the disciples who obeyed and got the colt for Jesus. They did the possible, and God did the impossible by providing a praise parade that fulfilled the Old Testament scriptures.

"We must keep on praying and waiting upon the Lord, until the sound of a mighty rain is heard. There is no reason why we should not ask for large things; and without doubt we shall get large things if we ask in faith, and have the courage to wait with patient perseverance upon Him, meantime doing those things which lie within our power to do."[15]

True Story: My Aunt Bettie was 35 and single when she was diagnosed with ovarian cancer. Not one to seek medical attention, Aunt Bettie had finally gone to a doctor, a family friend, because she felt like people at work were beginning to talk—after all, she looked very pregnant. Immediately following the examination, Dr. Kennedy insisted my aunt go straight to the hospital for surgery. After rushing through preparation procedures, a surgeon performed an operation to try to remove the large, malignant tumor in her abdomen.

In the waiting room after the surgery, Dr. Kennedy held back tearful emotion as she shared with my grandmother and other family members that while she, the assisting physician to the surgeon held the tumor carefully in her hands for removal, it burst and spread to the other organs in my aunt's abdomen. Dr. Kennedy sadly and regretfully shared the news that my Aunt Bettie had only 3 months to live. My grandmother assured the kind doctor that Jesus was going to heal her daughter. Doctor Kennedy went on to explain, if there was anything my aunt had ever dreamed of doing, this was the time to do it.

After the surgery, Aunt Bettie agreed to the cancer treatments the hospital recommended in an attempt to lengthen her life. Because of those treatments, Aunt Bettie lost her hair but not her sense of humor. She would regale us, her family, with funny stories of losing her wig at the most inopportune and embarrassing moments. Through it all, Aunt Bettie maintained her joy and her strong faith in God on a very difficult journey.

In between Aunt Bettie's treatments, my dad asked her and my grandmother to meet him at the Prayer and Bible Conference being held in Baton Rouge, Louisiana. The night my Aunt Bettie attended, she was invited to the platform where ministers gathered around her and prayed till it seemed Heaven heard. From then on, Aunt Bettie began feeling better with each new day. So much better, in fact, that she decided not to take any more cancer treatments. Doctor Kennedy later did tests and found every trace of cancer was gone. She assured my aunt there was nothing they, the medical staff, had done to cure her. At the writing of this book, Aunt Bettie is now 84 years old and has had excellent health since that day. She still joyously shares with others the miracle of God's healing in her life.

True Story: Captain Dale Black was the sole survivor in an airplane crash that took two lives. In his amazing book, *Flight to Heaven,* he shares about his experience of seeing Heaven, along with his miraculous spiritual transformation and physical recovery after the crash. His body was mangled, though miraculously he suffered no internal injuries. He was released from the hospital eight days after being admitted. However, in spite of those miracles, he was given little to no hope of recovery of his shattered ankle, the mobility of one shoulder due to an exploded socket, and his right eye, which was badly damaged.

In spite of those seeming impossibilities, God showed Dale how to exercise his faith by doing the possible. Each day, when no one was around, Dale would take the patch off of his injured eye, cover his good eye, and try to read his Bible. God used his obedience and restored his sight. The Lord also showed Dale how to hang his arm out of the car window and use the lift of the wind to exercise the muscles in his mangled shoulder. Once again, God used his obedience and brought a miracle. Finally, the matter of Dale's ankle, which had no blood flow and no hope of recovery had to be addressed. The doctor suggested surgery to fuse Dale's ankle to his leg, which would have prevented him from ever walking normally again. This time, the only solution was to walk by faith and fully trust God for His will to be accomplished. Dale refused the surgery. The end result was a miraculous restoration of his ankle. God gave Dale complete recovery, in spite of all of the impossible situations, against all odds.

SOMETHING TO THINK ABOUT: Remember the ten lepers Jesus healed (Luke 17:11-19)? Jesus simply told them, *"Go show yourselves to the priests." "As they went,"* the Bible says, *"they were cleansed."* As they obeyed Jesus' instructions to do what was possible on their part, God healed them. When we pray, Jesus will often give us a task. As with the lepers, sometimes there is a step of faith we must take. It may be we are to wait and trust. At other times, God gives us a task to improve us personally or help our progress. We may be directed to study a particular topic in the Word for insight or be instructed to write our journey. God knows the details of our story may help a friend in the future. Sometimes our job is to minister to someone else who is waiting for an answer from the Lord. Remember to trust God to do what only He can do.

PRAYER EXERCISE: Pray today that God will show you **what is possible for you to do** in your impossible situation. Sometimes, we don't receive the answer immediately. We must continue to seek God's heart and search His Word to get an answer to our question. Pray about this in the morning and in the evening, just before you go to sleep. Make a section in your journal for this exercise as evidence to the Lord that you have an expectation to hear from Him. God really does care and wants to speak to you about the issues of your life.

> *Romans 5:3b-5 We rejoice in our sufferings, knowing that suffering produces endurance, and endurance produces character, and character produces hope, and hope does not put us to shame, because God's love has been poured into our hearts through the Holy Spirit who has been given to us.*

Signs from Heaven

Isaiah 7:11 (NIV) Ask the Lord your God for a sign, whether in the deepest depths or in the highest heights.

"Beware in your prayers, above everything else, of limiting God, not only by unbelief, but by fancying that you know what He can do. Expect unexpected things above all that we ask or think."

-Andrew Murray

O ne day recently, a young lady who had been in our ministry a number of years ago came to my mind. I felt very sad because Elizabeth and I had lost contact. She had returned to Germany, and we had moved to Missouri. I realized I could not even remember her last name if I had wanted to contact her. I told the Lord I supposed I would have to wait to Heaven to find out about Elizabeth.

Miraculously, 3 days later, Elizabeth made contact with Bruce on his Facebook page. She had written me a short letter, sharing some good things that had happened in her life, and asked for me to contact her. I was thankful and totally amazed!

I said, "Lord, you answered a prayer I did not even have the faith to pray, and yet, things I have prayed countless times are yet unanswered." Inside, I heard this response from the Lord: "I did this so you would know I have heard your other prayers, though you have not seen the answers, yet."

Don't get me wrong. God does not want us to live each day requiring a sign from Him. Walking by faith is an important part of our spiritual journey. However, it is evident that God used signs to direct His people in both Old and New Testaments. When we are in a hard place and need assurance that God is hearing us, a sign in any area, even in seemingly small things, can spark confidence and assurance in us that He is hearing our prayers. It builds faith in our hearts that our other answers are on the way.

The children of Israel were faced with a terrorizing situation at the Red Sea. Though God had provided an angel and a pillar of fire behind them, they were well aware their enemy was still breathing down their necks on the other side of that protection—the barrier of the Red Sea was still before them. After Moses extended his rod and the waters parted, there was still work God had to do. *"And the Lord opened up a path through the water with a strong east wind. **The wind blew all that night,** turning the seabed into dry land"* (Exodus 14:21, NLT).

The children of Israel had to take comfort in the signs of intervention and protection that were evident before them, though the problem was not fully solved in one moment—God's work went on throughout the night. The same is true in the middle of your dark times. Jesus assures us in John 5:17 (NLT), *"My Father is always working, and so am I."*

Consider that Israel, upon leaving Egypt (as told in the book of Exodus), started their journey with the parting of the Red Sea and concluded it with the parting of the Jordan River, just before their conquests in the Promised Land. What if there had been no other evidence provided by God on their pilgrimage? Thankfully, God certainly did reveal Himself and His power time after time during that wilderness journey.

Likewise, God doesn't just begin a relationship with us and disregard us until Heaven. Scripture says He is "God with us" (Isaiah 7:14). He is present in our challenging situations, hearing and answering our prayers, lifting our heavy hearts when they are burdened, showing signs of His faithfulness all along our way. It may be a scripture, a word of encouragement, an improvement in the situation, or an incident that sparks Jesus' assurance in us. As you pray, God will confirm to you that He is working on each problem. God cares about you and wants to give you signs of hope on your journey, also.

True Story: During a time of prayer, my sister Ruth wrote in her journal several pages of words she felt were from God. Since they did not seem to fit her situation, she assumed they were for me or someone else in our family. Just a couple of weeks later, Ruth's husband went to be with the Lord during his recovery from a heart surgery. Neville's death really was such a shock to Ruth and to our whole family. It was very hard to understand the "why" behind his untimely death.

As Ruth was trying to make sense of it all, in those stark first few hours after her husband's death, she felt strongly impressed she should read from her journal. There in her last entry was the word the Lord had spoken so clearly. His words said Ruth was to trust Him. God promised my sister in those pages that He was going to turn her bleak and terrible situation around for something wonderful for her life.

God's comforting and assuring words have carried Ruth through the storm of grief and disillusionment the death of a spouse so often brings. She has been such a strong woman of faith in the midst of the difficult physical and emotional challenges of her life. God's word to Ruth in her journal has been a constant source of strength. It is a reminder not to fear the future. God will walk with us even through the "valley of the shadow" experiences.

True Story: My friend and prayer partner, Barb, has been such a faithful intercessor, and yet it seemed her prayers for her unsaved family would never be answered. We began to ask God for a sign that He was working and would answer her prayers. Around this same time, Barb went out of state to attend her granddaughter's graduation. While there, she became so sick she had to be taken to the emergency room and missed the graduation. Every test indicated emphysema. The x-rays revealed damage in both of Barb's lungs. She had experienced bouts of pneumonia and bronchitis in the past but had not known the extent of the damage.

Barb's friends and prayer partners began to cover her in prayer, seeking God for her healing. A couple of months later, Barb was retested. Her doctor called her to share the amazing results. "I am baffled," he said, as he explained the pulmonary function tests showed no damage. Barb's lungs were clear! She was able then to share her testimony with her doctor and her family of God's healing intervention. Though her other prayers have yet to be answered, it confirmed to Barb that God is indeed hearing her prayers about her family, also.

True Story: My friend, Pattie, was on a trip to South Korea to visit her daughter. She had been praying with me about a very challenging situation in my life, as had Bruce, who was on a ministry trip to Haiti. It was very difficult to be disconnected from the two people who had been praying with me so faithfully.

Several days had passed with no communication from Pattie. Since I previously received a short email or text from her each day during her travels, I had begun to be concerned for her safety. As I went to bed, I asked the Lord to please let me receive some correspondence from her. The next day, I received a text from Pattie saying she had a dream about me and felt impressed to get in contact with me. She explained that she had been on a trip to the mountains with no Internet connection. Pattie's dream brought comfort and confirmation to me that God was hearing my prayers.

SOMETHING TO THINK ABOUT: Are signs from God a biblical concept? God gave Noah the sign of a rainbow to assure him and his future generations that the Lord would never flood the earth again (Genesis 9:12-14). God gave signs to Abraham, Isaac, and Jacob. He gave many signs to Pharaoh, to Egypt, and to Israel, before and during their wanderings. Many times in the Old Testament, people sought a sign from God to know He would be with them in a battle or a challenging situation (Joshua, Gideon, Jonathan, David, Hezekiah, Nehemiah). Consider Isaiah's prophesy that God would give Israel a sign about their coming Messiah: *"The virgin shall conceive and bear a son, and shall call his name Immanuel"* (7:14). God gave many other signs to confirm the coming of Jesus, His Son.

There are times, as with Israel, God has been giving us signs of His faithfulness, but we haven't noticed or understood the implications of those signs. What has God done to confirm He is mindful of you and is hearing your prayers? As we keep a record of things God is doing in our lives, even the little ways that He is speaking in the midst of our journey, we find encouragement to go on trusting Him for the fulfillment of His promises to us.

PRAYER EXERCISE: Today, ask God to remind you of the different things He has already done in the past to assure you He is active in your present situation. As you go about your day, begin to tune in to the many ways God is speaking to you. It may be a scripture you read, a devotional that speaks assurance, a song that comes to mind or some words from a friend or your pastor. Remember to write these things in your prayer journal so you will remember them.

> *1 John 5:14,15 And this is the confidence that we have toward him, that if we ask anything according to his will he hears us. And if we know that he hears us in whatever we ask, we know that we have the requests that we have asked of him.*
>
> *Hebrews 4:16 "Let us then with confidence draw near to the throne of grace, that we may receive mercy and find grace to help in time of need."*

DON'T GIVE UP

Acts 1:7 He said to them, It is not for you to know times or seasons that the Father has fixed by his own authority.

Daniel 10:12 Then he said to me, "Fear not, Daniel, for from the first day that you set your heart to understand and humbled yourself before your God, your words have been heard and I have come because of your words."

Proverbs 20:24 (NLT) The Lord directs our steps, so why try to understand everything along the way?

"Just because you cannot see God working does not mean He is not at work."

-Adrian Rogers

My mother-in-law Jimmie Ruth prayed for her brother, Harry, for many years—all with no results. She often faced times of discouragement and felt like giving up. She would invite Harry to church for special events, hoping each one would be an opportunity for him to hear the gospel and surrender his life to Jesus. On one such occasion, just before she picked up the phone to invite him to a special service, she said to her family, "Oh, what's the use? He will never come!" My father-in-law Lamar encouraged her, "Just try one more time." Harry agreed to go to church that night, and it was in that very church service God radically saved him!

There are times when we have diligently prayed about something, yet it seems a worthless effort. We see no sign that God is hearing, much less responding to our need. It is so easy for us to stop praying and give up.

We all face those times—even the prophet Daniel—a man who was known for his faithful prayers (Daniel 6:10). In Daniel, chapter 10, the prophet was in a time of humbling himself before God with fasting. For three weeks, he had received no indication that Heaven heard.

Daniel was seeing no evidence, but God had already commissioned a response to his prayers (Daniel 10:12). Finally, the angel Gabriel visited Daniel and shared the reason for God's apparent delay. Intense warfare occurring in the heavenly realms required extra forces for Daniel's prayers to be answered (Daniel 10:13). Thankfully, the prophet had prayerfully persisted, despite the lack of evidence.

There are times we, too, have prayed—even fasted—but we see nothing. We hear nothing. It is not a time to give up, though. You and I must persist in prayer! Like Daniel, we don't know what battles are being waged in heavenly realms. In spite of our questions, we can be assured, if we are praying—God is working— simply because we can take Him at His Word.

What about situations and circumstances that make no sense? Daniel faced this also. He lived in Babylon as a Jewish exile during the Babylonian captivity. Forced to leave his homeland and his people, Daniel faced situations of disillusionment and even life-threatening challenges (like a lions' den), but he did not give up on God. He kept on faithfully trusting and praying.

While in Babylon, God sent Gabriel to reveal future events to Daniel—specifically, the prophetic timeline of humanity, future events in Heaven, and the times of the Great Tribulation on Earth. None of these things made sense to Daniel. He said, *"I heard, but I did not understand"* (Daniel 12:8). When he asked about the outcome of the events in the vision, Gabriel simply said, "Go your way, Daniel, for the words are shut up and sealed until the time of the end."

How does this story relate to my situation, you may ask? Like Daniel, we have received many heavenly truths: We have been given the message of salvation (1John 5:11-12, Acts 4:12). We have been entrusted with knowledge that the prophets longed to understand (1 Peter 1:10,11; Matthew 13:17). We have been given things angels long to look into (1 Peter 1:12). In spite of all of those amazing spiritual truths, you and I still don't have all of the answers on this side of Heaven. When circumstances in our lives don't make sense, we can lose heart and even begin to fear.

It is in these times—when everything we have known becomes the unknown—that we must embrace what I call the "name, rank and serial number" of the Christian. When the Enemy's voice comes to torment you and take you captive with his lies— stand firm and repeat, ***"I know the one in whom I trust, and I am sure that he is able to guard what I have entrusted to him until the day of his return"*** *(2 Timothy 1:12, NLT)* .

These words of the Apostle Paul, imprisoned in a Roman prison cell, are a stabilizer much like the words a soldier in our military verbalizes when taken into captivity. They are our pledge of ultimate trust, committing our lives and our concerns to our loving Father. He hears and He is answering every prayer. God will bring you through your captivity as you keep on praying and trusting.

True Story: My friend, Kimberly, walked through a judicial nightmare. She was falsely accused of a hit and run accident by her neighbors. It was a frame-up. Since Kimberly had been a celebrated teacher in the public school system for many years, the media jumped in to try to make it a gigantic spread. Her face was in the paper and on the nightly news. She endured harassment by law enforcement. She went through days of persecution and months of incrimination. She suffered the shame and embarrassment of having her reputation and name publicly smeared. It was hard to understand. Kimberly had served God so faithfully in her private life and in the public arena. How could this be happening? It didn't make sense.

In the midst of the trial, God gave Kimberly amazing favor. The Lord held her job steady. Kimberly's principal and the school board backed her up as an innocent citizen. Parents and students rallied around her. During this time, she and her school choir received a celebrated honor and were privileged to sing at a statewide teachers' convention. There, my friend received a standing ovation.

Yet, most days it felt like the hard journey would never end. During these long days and difficult months, Kimberly's friends and church family prayed earnestly for her. God laid it upon my heart to gather other trusted prayer partners to intercede for her. He gave me scriptures to share with Kimberly upon which to stand. Bruce and I claimed the Word of God together in prayer with my friend and her husband, Monte.

It was a challenging prayer journey and a grueling trust walk. Finally, the district attorney, for lack of evidence, dropped Kimberly's case, and all charges and accusations were expunged (all traces removed) from her records. The end was an overwhelming victory!

True Story: Bruce and I were in the small town of Pulaski, Tennessee, for an outreach sponsored by the Convoy of Hope and the churches in that area to help the poor of their community. As we were chatting with some of the helpers in a small kitchen area, the conversation turned to Cajun food. Bruce shared that, though Texan by birth, I was raised in the New Orleans area. One lady brightened up as she revealed that she was raised on the west bank of New Orleans. Surprised, I shared that I was also raised in that area of the city. Tears came to my eyes as we narrowed our connection further, realizing she and her grandmother had attended the church my dad had pastored. I shared with Liz how week after week her dear grandmother would stop me and ask me as a teenager to pray with her. There in the church aisle, we would stop and pray for her children and grandchildren to be saved, calling them each by name. Those prayers for Liz, prayed to the Lord many years before in New Orleans, were fulfilled in Pulaski, Tennessee, in answer to her grandmother Josephine Tabor's many prayers.

SOMETHING TO THINK ABOUT: God cares about your life, your family, and your future even more than you do. He is actively working to answer your prayers. Consider that God is delaying the coming of Jesus because He doesn't want anyone (including those you are praying for) to miss Heaven. Our loving Father desires all to come to repentance (2 Peter 3:9). Regardless of your greatest prayer obstacle, keep on praying in faith!

God can be trusted with the answers, solutions, and outcomes that we do not yet have in our understanding or possession. We must pray earnestly, serve Him faithfully, and leave the timing of the answers to Him. In the meantime, we can rest assured our prayers are making a difference. Prayer changes people, prayer changes circumstances, and prayer changes us.

PRAYER EXERCISE: As you pray today, commit each of your loved ones and your burdens of concern to Jesus. Record them by name in your journal. Alongside each name or concern write: "Lord, you are working and I am trusting. "Speak aloud each name and situation to God in prayer with your declaration of full trust in God. Remember, the result of your full trust will be God's peace.

> *Isaiah 26:3 You keep him in perfect peace whose mind is stayed on you, because he trusts in you.*

> *Psalm 37:5 Commit your way to the Lord, Trust also in Him, And He shall bring it to pass.*

Get in the Race

1 Corinthians 9:24-26 (NLT) Don't you realize that in a race everyone runs, but only one person gets the prize? So run to win! All athletes are disciplined in their training. They do it to win a prize that will fade away, but we do it for an eternal prize. So I run with purpose in every step.

"Spiritual work is taxing work and men are loath to do it. Praying, true praying costs an outlay of serious attention and of time, which flesh and blood do not relish."

-E.M. Bounds

Let's go back to the story of Roger Bannister in the first chapter. Every great accomplishment in life comes in spite of some degree of struggle and disadvantage. Roger Bannister's immortal sub 4-minute mile certainly evidenced that. Consider the number of things that could have prevented his achievement that day:

- He was not a prodigy born with an incredible talent for running. In fact, Roger did not become serious about running until he was 17 years old and entering Oxford University, where he barely made the university's third track team.
- Roger regularly trained only about seven times a week unlike the two-a-day workouts of most athletes of our time. His medical studies also occupied a great deal of his focus.
- Roger did not run on a new synthetic fast track. The less than ideal surface Roger ran on for his most notable race was a cinder track, which created resistance making for a slower run.
- The day of his amazing victory, he had not run a race in 8 months since there was no such thing as an indoor running track. In his day, no races happened until Spring.

- The weather was much less than perfect the day of the race. Near gale-force winds delayed the starting time and threatened to stop the event. Even during the race, the wind was a formidable factor with which he had to contend.
- Medical experts of his day espoused that it was physically impossible for the human heart to withstand such a feat. As a medical student, it must have been a matter for serious contemplation.
- No other runner had ever gone below 4 minutes in the 1-mile run. Few believed it was even a possibility. It was a psychological hurdle Roger had to mentally overcome.

We all have disadvantages

What is keeping you from winning the race of prayer? Does it feel like an impossible task? Do you have trouble staying focused? Do you feel like you have no legacy to fall back on or feel alone in your endeavor? Is your home environment not conducive to quiet times of prayer? Is your schedule a rat race? Do you tend to give up when answers are not forthcoming?

None of these things are the final word on prayer. Remember, every race has hurdles of some sort. Begin by asking God to help you to be victorious over your obstacles. Developing strategies to incorporate prayer into your life takes persistence, but you can do it! Make Jesus a lifelong partner in finding what works best for you.

Open yourself to the strategies mentioned in this book: quiet time with God, a prayer journal, prayer partnerships, prayer stations, prayer walks, or prayer exercises. A fresh, serious mentality was the impetus that jumpstarted Roger Bannister into his success as a runner. A fresh outlook and new inspiration can also help you win at your race in the realm of prayer.

In a *heavenly* sense, those who have laid the groundwork of prayer—our Savior, the prophets, the apostles, the great men and women of faith throughout history—surround you and me in the "grandstand" as we prepare to run our race (Hebrews,

188

chapters 11; 12:1). In a *spiritual* sense, we are also surrounded by those who have prayed for us on our individual journeys to faith in Christ. They have passed the baton on to you and me.

Now it is our turn to pray for those closest to us, for the church at large, for the lost people of our world, and for the issues of this generation of which we are a part. It is our time in history to rise up and make a difference through prayer.

We have purpose and destiny endowed by God. We must rid ourselves of everything that is a hindrance, be it sin, distraction, or negligence. The Enemy will do his best to stop us by making us feel overwhelmed, incompetent, incapable, unqualified, and unworthy. We must resist him and persevere.

It is time for us to look to the Author and Finisher of our faith: Jesus. He is the One who started us on this race in the first place and He is the only One who can help us get to the finish line. After all, that is exactly what prayer is all about!

> *Hebrews 12:1,2a (NLT) "Therefore, since we are surrounded by such a huge crowd of witnesses to the life of faith, let us strip off every weight that slows us down, especially the sin that so easily trips us up. And let us run with endurance the race God has set before us. We do this by keeping our eyes on Jesus, the champion who initiates and perfects our faith."*

APPENDIX

Day 15

According to the New Testament, at the moment of our salvation, the Holy Spirit comes to live in us (1 Corinthians 3:16; 2 Corinthians 1:22; Romans 8:9; Ephesians 1:14). His *indwelling* is, according to these scriptures, a confirmation of our salvation.

However, Jesus taught if we ask for the ***gift of the Holy Spirit***, the Father would give Him to us (Luke 11:13). Since asking for this "gift" was not part of the instructions of Christ or the Apostles in order to receive salvation, we must ask ourselves, to what gift was Jesus referring? It would appear from other references He was indicating the baptism or *infilling* of the Holy Spirit (Acts 2:4).

As recorded in Acts chapter 2, the Holy Spirit filled believers, and they spoke with tongues on the Day of Pentecost. Amazingly, the term "the gift of the Holy Spirit" is mentioned specifically within that chapter in reference to this outpouring (2:38). Three subsequent times the term "gift of the Holy Spirit" is used when believers were filled with the Spirit throughout the book of Acts (8:20; 10:45; 11:17). Paul, in the book of Ephesians, instructed believers, to *"be filled with the Spirit"* (5:18). Since the Father has made provision for all believers, it is up to us to ask Him for the gift of the infilling of His Spirit.

Here are some books to read to learn more about being filled with the Holy Spirit:

Holy Spirit, Agent of Change by Dr. Lynn W. Aurich

Tongues, the Language of the Supernatural by Janet Brazee

Be Filled with the Spirit by Dr. Doyle Jones

Pentecost: This Story is Our Story by Robert P. Menzies

Have You Received the Holy Spirit Since You Believed? By Lloyd Singley

Day 19

Prayer Alignment Stretch

Begin by standing against a wall to establish good posture. Step forward from the wall.

Step 1. Stretch arms outward from the body at sides, forming a cross. (Pray for the world: for the lost, for government leaders, for the enslaved, for the incarcerated, for the poor, for orphans and widows, for the hurting and broken.)

Step 2. Form a W position by bending arms at elbows, palms of hands facing up and forward. (Pray for the church, both local and worldwide, for purity, unity, renewal, for ministers, for lay leaders, for the suffering church.)

Step 3. Form a V position by straightening and extending arms upward at a slant. (Pray for your extended family. Include prayer for the unsaved, for generational issues and relational issues.)

Step 4. Form a U position by extending arms straight above head. (Pray for the needs and issues of your immediate family. Pray for salvation, for unity, for holiness.)

Step 5. Form an I position by keeping arms extended above your head, palms together. (Pray for your marriage to be filled with love, faithfulness, understanding, unity, joy, and peace. Pray also for specific things your spouse needs or is facing.)

Step 6. Form a traditional prayer pose by lowering arms, keeping palms together and elbows angled out. (Pray for yourself for guidance, for healing of spirit, soul, and body and for the destiny of God to be fulfilled in your life.)

Step 7. Raise both arms and give praise to God.

NOTES

[1] Megan Erickson, Benefits of prayer "Is The Human Brain Hardwired for God?" www.bigthink.com.

[2] Bob Beltz, Becoming a Man of Prayer, (Navpress 1996), p. 46

[3] Brother Lawrence, The Practice of the Presence of God

[4] Charles A. Miles, In the Garden, 1913, (*Commons Public Domain*)

[5] C. J. Ellicott, A Bible Commentary for English Readers, (Forgotten Books Publishing)

[6] Guillermo Gonzalez and Jay W. Richards, The Privileged Planet, (Publishing Inc. Washington, D.C. 2004).

[7] R.A. Torey on George Muller, "The Power of Prayer," (Zondervan Publishing) p.81.

[8] John Maxwell, Partners in Prayer, (Thomas Nelson), page 39.

[9] George O. Otis, Jr., Video, "Transformations", http://www.sentinelgroup.org.

[10] Cindy Trimm, The Art of War for Spiritual Battle, (Charisma House, 2010), pp.19-24 James H. O'Neill, "The True Story of the Patton Prayer" (Review of the News, Oct 6,1971), first appearing as a government document in 1950, http://www.pattonhq.com/prayer.html

[11] Andrew Murray, The Best of Andrew Murray, (Baker Publishing Group), p. 143

[12] The Center for Global Christianity, based at Gordon Conwell Seminary, www.globalchristianity.org/globalcontext.

[13] Linda J. Waite and Evelyn L. Lehrer, The Benefits from Marriage and Religion in the United States: A Comparative Analysis

[14] Lettie Cowman, Streams in the Desert, March 22, (Zondervan Publishing}

[15] Lettie Cowman, Streams in the Desert, March 22, (Zondervan Publishing}